DUCKS IN DETENTION

Ducks in Detention

by
JOHN TERRY
C.Biol., M.I.Biol., M.I.Hort., A.R.Ag.S., F.R.S.A.

illustrated by
HENRY BREWIS

Farming Press

First published 1990

British Library Cataloguing in Publication Data

Terry, John, *1952*–
  Ducks in detention.
  1. Rural conditions—Study and teaching
  (Secondary)—England
  I. Title
  630'.7'1242   S535.G7

  ISBN 0-85236-208-0

Published by Farming Press Books
4 Friars Courtyard, 30–32 Princess Street
Ipswich IP1 1RJ, United Kingdom

Distributed in North America
by Diamond Farm Enterprises,
Box 537, Alexandria Bay, NY 13607, USA

Typeset by Galleon Photosetting, Ipswich
Reproduced, printed and bound in Great Britain by
Mackays of Chatham PLC, Chatham, Kent

Charlie

IT WAS getting towards the end of April, and so towards the end of the lambing season. Most of the ewes and lambs at school were going out to the paddocks in the daytime and returning to the buildings in the evening. However, the grass was rapidly being eaten and the sheep needed moving.

In previous years, Lord Clifton had been good enough to let us keep our ewes and lambs on his estate which was about eight miles away from the school. I telephoned him and asked if the sheep could come and spend their summer holidays with him.

He readily agreed and suggested I use the one-acre paddock at the rear of the house.

'I must pay a rent this year,' I said. It seemed to me that our sheep had had enough free vacations over the years.

'Oh, the rent will be little or nothing,' his lordship replied.

Now I always like to get something for nothing, but I did not have the cheek to agree with him this time, so I offered him half a lamb for his freezer. It would be ready about August time. Of course it would not be one of our Kerry Hill show sheep. I was not going to have one of those slaughtered for the table.

Lord Clifton was in accord with the offer and so next day after school I took three of my pupils, Carol, Jo and Michael, over to Lord Clifton's farm. Carol was a tall girl for her age and, although only in the third year, looked older – a joker if ever there was one. Michael was also a third-year pupil but very small and pasty-faced. He had a frail look about him which made people who did not know him wonder how long he was destined for this world; but Michael belied his appearance and was, in fact, as tough as old army boots. Jo was only a second-year pupil but was a most enthusiastic participant in rural studies – a very open, friendly type of girl.

Lord Clifton's abode boasted two drives. The main drive, for visitors and guests, swept majestically up to the imposing front door of the country house. The second drive, a smaller affair, was for farm workers and tradesmen. Although still well maintained, it was not as regal as the main drive and meandered past the farm cottage, farm buildings and up to the back door

2

of the big house.

'Are we going up the main drive?' asked Michael with some awe.

'No. We're the peasants,' said pack joker Carol before I could get a word in edgeways.

I instinctively turned into the back drive. There is a spinney on one side and fields on the other. One of the fields was showing a thriving crop of wheat but the fence that separated the wheat field from our small paddock was in such a bad state of repair that it did not look stock proof and I did not fancy getting a hefty bill from his lordship for a ruined crop. Job number one – mend the fence.

We passed the farm cottage on our left and a welter of memories came flooding back. My aunt and uncle had lived there for about thirty years when they managed the estate and, as a girl, my mother used to spend her weekends and holidays with them. Later, when I was old enough, I did likewise. Hence my love of farming.

Nowadays it is occupied by another couple – it will never be quite the same again. If only we could turn the clock back. I was totally lost in my reverie but brought abruptly to earth by the honking noise of the geese. There were about twenty surrounding our parked vehicle; they belonged to her ladyship and as geese go they never struck me as being very fierce – certainly not in the same class as our Gregory and his wives.

I told my pupils not to worry about these geese and to follow me. I pointed to 'our' paddock and was about to stride over when we were confronted by a huge dog. He bounded over to us and immediately jumped up Michael. He was friendly and wanted some fuss. This was their introduction to Charlie – a golden labrador type of dog plus a doubtful mixture of a number of breeds – a street hybrid.

'I didn't know his lordship had got a dog,' remarked Jo.

'Oh yes,' I replied. 'Charlie is a stray he took in.'

We started walking towards our field, Charlie running and romping in front of us.

It was a struggle to actually get into our paddock. It had a heavy gate which had never been put on hinges – it was tied in place with string. After trying to open it with a bit of fun and games of 'It's a Knockout' standard we found it was a damn sight easier to climb over. Charlie squeezed through the bars and ran excitedly in front.

There was plenty of grass in the field but we acquired a couple of squatters. Two of her ladyship's hunters had broken into our paddock after knocking down some of the fencing from the 'top field' as it is called; there they were contentedly eating our grass.

We all went over and checked the fence more closely – it certainly needed some work doing on it. I had not been organised enough to bring any tools or fencing materials so it would mean another trip the next day if it was fine.

After school the next day, we hitched the trailer to the car, loaded up a few fencing rails, found our trusty hammer and some nails, and the four of us went back to the farm.

Again we were greeted by fussy Charlie who bounded into the paddock with us. The horses had moved back into the top field of their own accord, so the planned wild west round-up was abandoned, saving us quite a bit of valuable time. The fencing posts were fine but the horses had knocked down some rails; we did the best job we could – without spending too much money, I may add. We had almost finished when Lord Clifton walked over to us.

'Hello, all of you,' he said in his very distinct and clear Eton accent. We all said hello, but before we could say anything else he went on, 'Those dratted horses of her ladyship's; they are damn things – sorry they caused you a spot of trouble – I wouldn't bother with them you know – don't like horses much – I'd sooner have the cattle.'

I did not wish to take sides as the last thing I wanted was her ladyship falling out with me, so I said nothing and just smiled.

'You have made a first-class job of the fencing,' he said. We talked farming for five minutes and then Jo asked him how Charlie the stray had been found.

'Well, one of my workers, Ivor, was ploughing the twenty-four acre, that's the long field next to the road – you came past it on the way here – damned difficult field to plough I must say, it's very stiff clay you know. Anyhow, back to the main story – now, where was I? Oh yes – there's a lay-by, it's a nuisance – people drop litter and much of it ends up in my fields, some people use it as a rubbish tip, even throw their junk over my hedges. We've had everything from a dead cat to an old bike and not to mention of course, that some use it as a toilet. I'm wandering off the main track again. This particular day Ivor noticed a car in the lay-by, it only stopped for a minute or two then took off at high speed. Ivor carried on ploughing and as he got nearer

the hedge he noticed a puppy – it ran through the
hedge. It was a large puppy – probably three or four
months old. Ivor stopped the tractor and tried to catch
it but the dog ran across the road and he lost sight of
it. Then, about a week later I got up one morning and

found the pup lying on my doorstep. He looked like a young fox, so I called him Charlie.'

'Where had the dog been all that time?' asked Jo.

'Roaming around, scavenging out of dustbins no doubt. He was certainly very dirty, thin and hungry.'

'It was good of you to take him in,' continued Jo.

'I couldn't bear to see the little mite in that state so I took him in, fed him, gave him a bed and he's been with us ever since. We think the world of him.'

His lordship said goodbye and set off with his dog towards the top field.

'Charlie is a lovely dog. How could his owners do such a horrible thing?' Jo asked of me.

'Perhaps they just got fed up with him or the novelty wore off. Maybe he was making a mess.'

'Or chewing furniture or slippers, or perhaps he was too expensive to feed,' butted in Michael.

'Or – or – they wanted to go on holiday and couldn't be bothered to put him in kennels,' chimed in Carol.

My pupils had already had one lesson from me on impulse buying, especially where pets are concerned. People buy an animal without thinking it through or discussing it with the rest of the family. They buy first, probably spotting it in a pet shop window, get home and realise they have not got even the basic equipment. No collar, no lead, no bed and no idea about feeding requirements. One of my aims in rural studies is to get the pupils to understand the commitment and dedication needed in keeping animals – these pupils had got the right idea.

'Lord Clifton ended it all happily though. I like a happy ending,' said Carol sentimentally.

'He's a lucky dog now,' said Michael, 'living in that

enormous mansion and with five hundred acres to run around in.'

'Yes,' I replied. 'He has his dinner on a silver dish and he's got baby blankets from Mothercare in his basket.'

'I'll swap places with him any day, Sir,' said Michael enviously. 'He could live in our semi and I could live here.'

'That's a lovely story,' said Carol. '*Charlie Comes From Rags To Riches*. I could write a book – or it would make a good film for children,' she said happily.

'Someone's already done it,' said Michael scathingly. 'It's called Lassie.'

We tidied up, then carried the unused fencing rails back to the trailer along with the hammer, saw and box of nails.

The next day we returned with some fertiliser – a compound fertiliser containing nitrogen, phosphorus and potassium. Once the sheep had finished the grass we would apply straight nitrogen again and then more nitrogen later in the season.

We did not possess a tractor or fertiliser spreader and so the fertiliser would have to be put on by hand. I use flower pots as markers. I mark out a couple of strips and then fill a bucket with fertiliser. I then put it on as if I am feeding free-range hens. I get the pupils to mark a new strip with some more flower pots, then they keep moving the pots to make more strips. Over the years I have become quite adept at the job and can apply it evenly. If you do not put it on evenly it shows when the grass grows. The parts that have been fertilised grow lush and green, the parts missed are almost bald. So there you are with a patchwork lawn or field.

Not a pretty sight.

A week later we took ten ewes and their fifteen lambs over to their new pasture. The grass by this time was plenty long enough for sheep and it really needed grazing off. I would check the flock two or three times a week; there was certainly no need for me to travel over every day because Lord Clifton would check them twice a day for me.

Just over a fortnight later Lord Clifton telephoned me at home. I had just returned from a show. Our sheep had won and I was, as they say, over the moon.

Lord Clifton's phone call burst the bubble.

'John – I've got some bad news for you,' he said, his voice full of concern.

'What is it?' I asked cautiously. I had a nasty premonition.

'A dog has been in the paddock and killed one of your lambs. He's chased the flock around and another one of the lambs is slightly injured.'

'Oh no,' I groaned. My heart sank. The joy of winning the show had all the shine taken off it.

'If I were you I'd fetch the sheep back tomorrow – wouldn't want it to happen again.'

His cultured tones rang out loud and clear. I thanked him. In a fuddled state of mind I rang my three young shepherds. Carol and Michael were available but Jo was out. I went without my tea. I think it would have choked me. With heavy heart I drove to school and hitched up the trailer. I was determined to fetch the sheep back there and then, and not leave it until morning.

Carol and Michael both cycled to school and within twenty minutes we were on the road. We were all shell-shocked and hardly spoke a word during the journey. We could not wait to get to the farm.

Lord Clifton had put the lamb in a hessian sack. I tipped it out onto the grass. Sadly, it was a little ewe lamb. She had got teeth marks on her neck and throat and at the top of her left hind leg. There was obviously nothing we could do so we put her back in the sack. We then got the rest of the flock into a farm building at the corner of our field. I examined the injured lamb, another ewe. She was not too bad – a few teeth marks on her neck and some tufts of wool missing. She was badly shaken and trembled with fear, but otherwise seemed all right.

I backed the trailer up to the building and loaded half the ewes and lambs on the top deck and the other half on the bottom. I went back to the dead lamb for a closer examination.

'It's a big dog by the size of those teeth marks,' I said.

'Let's see,' said Michael, pushing in and screwing his face up in distaste.

'It's certainly got a huge jaw – look at the pattern of teeth marks,' said Carol. 'I've been thinking,' she continued. 'I don't really like to mention it but the zoo is only a couple of miles up the road – what if it's a lion or tiger that's escaped.'

'Yes,' said Michael, 'it could be lying watching us waiting to pounce.'

With dusk falling and the tall trees standing stark and black against the afterglow, their branches pointing like a million accusing fingers, it was getting a little spooky. The nocturnal creatures were emerging for their nightly forage and sounds unnoticed during the daytime were amplified a hundredfold on the clear night air. Twigs cracked like pistol shots, leaves rustled menacingly as if some unseen paws were padding stealthily through them. I felt an icy shudder go down my back. Imagination is a powerful emotion and these two did not help matters. The conversation was rapidly degenerating towards werewolves, vampires and flesh-eating zombies. I am normally a very rational chap but this pair were beginning to get to me. Time for Sir to put things back in perspective.

'A man-eating tiger is highly unlikely,' I said with more confidence than I felt.

'I'm still frightened,' said Carol. 'And what about a man-eating lion? You haven't said that's unlikely.'

'Carol,' I said sternly, 'look – the animal didn't eat the lamb did it? So it can't be a lion or tiger. They kill for food.'

'I don't know,' chipped in Michael. 'Tigers kill for the devil of it.' I could have cheerfully killed him at that moment.

Suddenly a tawny owl hooted very loudly, adding to the eerie atmosphere.

'Let's go home s-s-sir. Please,' stuttered Carol.

I like to hear owls calling and subconsciously I knew we were in no danger. We got back into the car and towed the trailer back into the farmyard. The white geese stood out in silhouette against the pitch-black yard – like a black-and-white negative. Lord Clifton appeared and could not apologise enough. But we could not hold him responsible.

It was a very dejected trio that made the return journey to the school. All thoughts of our earlier triumph had been pushed from our minds. We were thoroughly fed up. It was a good ewe lamb that had been killed – certainly one we would have kept for breeding purposes. Back at school we bathed the injured lamb's wounds and injected her with antibiotics. The bereaved mother had no other lamb so I would have to keep her inside – off the lush grass – so that her milk would dry up. Later on that evening I telephoned another farmer and explained the situation to him. He agreed that the ewes and lambs could go to his farm temporarily.

The following day I telephoned Lord Clifton to see if he had sighted the dog. He had not. However, he had put the word out in the neighbourhood and he felt sure it would be the talk of the village hostelry that evening.

If a dog is caught red-pawed sheep-worrying the farmer is, by law, entitled to shoot on sight. Some farmers will try to catch the dog and trace the owner. Others will just let fly with a double-barrel shotgun.

The dog could be some child's pet, perfectly happy and well behaved at home, playing with children and sitting by the fire – but all the time leading a Jekyll-and-Hyde existence. Once a dog has experienced the thrill of the chase and tasted warm sheep blood it is even chances it will strike again.

Lord Clifton did not telephone me but I rang him about a fortnight later. There was no news of a stray dog or anyone else in the district losing sheep in that way.

A month went by and there were no reports of stray dogs.

'Bring your sheep back,' said Lord Clifton. 'There's so much grass here it wants eating. It looks as if your incident was a one-off occurrence. Obviously a stray dog that has left the district – no one has seen anything out of the ordinary.'

I agreed to bring the sheep back but added that I would like to put electric netting around the edge of the field. It probably would not stop a dog jumping over but it would give it something to think about before trying again. A shock through a cold, wet nose would not harm the dog but it might act as a deterrent. Lord Clifton thought it a good idea and with his reassurance we took the ewes and lambs back. Lord Clifton promised to check them each evening.

I actually checked them for one evening only – the first. They were fine. However, the next lunchtime the telephone rang.

'Hello, it's Lord Clifton here. I'm afraid I've got some very bad news for you.'

I broke out in a cold sweat. I knew without being told that the dog had paid a return visit and done some damage. He continued, 'One of my workers, Bill, heard a dog bark and ran into the field but he was too late – a lamb lay dead in one of the far corners. John, I'm so sorry but it was my dog, Charlie. He was running around and barking like a mad thing. Bill called Charlie to him and he stopped running the sheep and came over. Bill grabbed him by the collar and marched him around to me, then of course, he told the story to her ladyship and myself.'

'Oh surely not. Not Charlie.'

'Yes, I'm afraid so, John. But you can rest assured I've done the correct, in fact the only, thing that had to be done.'

I knew what was coming.

'I put Charlie in the car, took him to the vet and had him destroyed.'

'I am sorry to hear this,' I replied. I could tell by his lordship's voice that he was very upset. I started to feel guilty – it was our sheep that had caused Charlie's downfall.

Lord and Lady Clifton thought the world of Charlie. He was their 'baby', and now he was dead.

'I can't believe it,' I replied. I was stunned. 'I wish you had telephoned me first. I would have taken the temptation away. I certainly didn't want him to be put down.'

'No, John,' replied Lord Clifton, now with a more stern approach. 'My worker Bill saw it happen. If I had done nothing about it he would have gone down to the pub tonight and told everyone that I was harbouring a killer dog.'

'Yes I suppose so, but. . . .' Before I could say any more Lord Clifton carried on.

'No "buts", John. Once he has done this he will do it again and again – he could travel for miles, come across some sheep and attack.'

'But did Bill actually see Charlie kill the lamb?' I asked.

'No he didn't. But it's obvious – there are no other dogs here – it has got to be him – he was running and barking – all the evidence is against him.'

'I feel awful about the whole thing,' I replied.

'Well don't, John. There is no room for a dog like that in the countryside.'

'I feel sorry for her ladyship and yourself, though. I know how much you thought of him.'

14

'Well yes, thank you John. We are both upset. But what's done is done, and your sheep will be safe now.'

They were his lordship's final words on the matter.

I broke the news to my pupils – not just the three that had been involved – but I told the story to all my classes as well. Like me, they were shocked and some of them found it difficult, almost impossible, to accept that Charlie had been a rogue dog.

After school, Michael, Carol and Jo went over to the farm with me to collect the dead lamb and to check the others. There were teeth marks on the neck and throat, similar to those on the lamb that had been killed previously.

We put the dead lamb in the boot of the car – it was another good ewe lamb. It would not have been kept for showing but would have been sold off for breeding. We also caught the lamb's mother. Again it was a single lamb and the ewe would have to be dried off. My pupils were very down. I told them to go and look at Lord Clifton's calves while I went to find him.

I found him in the house. He only repeated what he had said on the telephone, that our sheep would be safe now and I could sleep soundly and go back to checking the flock twice a week instead of every day.

Life was still hectic but then it always was. I did not seem to get a minute, what with teaching, farming and giving talks.

Four days later the telephone rang again. It was teatime. Lord Clifton was at the other end.

15

'I hardly know how to tell you this, John. You have two more dead lambs – killed by a dog again, but we haven't seen it.'

I felt numb. 'That's incredible – unbelievable,' I gasped.

'Believe it, John. But this makes it look as if Charlie was not entirely to blame. He could have been working with another dog – a two-dog team. On the other hand he could have been completely innocent. Come and see for yourself.'

I told Lord Clifton I would be there straight away. I left my half-eaten tea (again) and telephoned my three pupils, only to find them all out. So, on my own, I drove to school, hitched up the trailer and trundled off to the farm once more.

Again the two lambs – one a ram, the other a ewe – had teeth marks on their necks and throats. I was just examining them when Lord Clifton came into the field.

'It's a mystery, John,' he said. 'I'm sorry to say, but it looks as if I jumped the gun with Charlie. He perhaps wasn't the only culprit. As I mentioned earlier, there could have been a two-dog team. But somehow I don't think so. I tell you what I think. I've got this feeling that Charlie was the good dog. I think he was chasing off the real killer – he was the hero really, but Bill saw only Charlie and not this other dog. I think Charlie was probably protecting the flock and for doing it I had him destroyed. I feel terrible about the whole business.' I could see that his lordship was still somewhat distraught.

'So do I,' I said emphatically. I was feeling properly browned-off by now. Two more dead lambs making a total of four in all, and a lovely dog which should never have been destroyed.

Lord Clifton and I got all the other sheep in. I checked them and found they were unharmed. We loaded the sheep into the trailer.

A month later Lord Clifton invited me over to his party one Sunday lunchtime. It was a splendid affair with only champagne to drink and, of course, the food was excellent. After we had eaten Lord Clifton took me to one side and gave me an envelope with instructions not to open it until I got home.

When I did open it – at home – I found it contained £160. Compensation for the four dead lambs.

I telephoned him to thank him and said he should not have done it as we did not know who the real killer was. He would have none of it, insisting we keep the money. This was very generous of him. We certainly appreciated it as it went to feed our ever-hungry livestock.

I do not suppose we shall ever know what really

happened. Charlie, it seemed, was a good, reliable and faithful dog. Like Lord Clifton I think he was protecting the flock, and for his efforts he suffered a gross miscarriage of justice.

Lord Clifton has since bought a black-and-white border collie puppy. His name is Midge and he really is a little beauty with all the shepherding instincts bred into him.

I have not used the paddock at Lord Clifton's again. It is a lovely pasture, but it is just not worth the risk.

Never a Dull Moment

SIR, ISN'T it time we had a dairy cow?' asked Carol.

'I have thought about it, I would like one but we haven't the room,' I replied.

'Sell a few of those Kerry Hill sheep, Sir. Then we would have the room.'

'Yes we could, but we stand more chance of breeding some prize-winners with a flock of twenty breeding ewes than four or so.' Sell the Kerry Hills? I would not hear of it.

'We wouldn't have to sell that many,' was her sensible reply.

'Probably not,' I answered. 'Another acre of grass is what we want.'

'But we have got half an acre of grass here and we could always rent some more.' One thing about Carol, she could stand her ground in an argument.

'Well, I'll think about it but I expect the answer will be no.'

People often remark, 'Your life never has a dull moment. Your pigs get out and cause trouble, your rams escape and get somebody else's ewes in lamb, and you seem to get into lots of scrapes and adventures.'

To some extent this is true. I do have more adventures – or misadventures – than most school staff. It is not all up and running, although I have done my fair share of that; but I can truthfully say life is never dull.

Never work with animals or children is an old show-biz adage but I disagree with that. I have worked with a combination of both for fifteen years – we have had some fun and we have caused some fun.

Animals often have no respect for people. If a ram decides he wants some of your damsons he is not averse to a bit of scrumping, as we found out with Harry the Hoover. He helped himself to hundreds, giving himself a king-size stomach-ache in the process, but it did not deter him from going back next day for seconds. When we finally caught him red-hoofed, so to speak, he was halfway up the tree nibbling them delicately off the branches.

Some of our calves took it into their heads to stage the Calgary Stampede along the school corridors and there was no chance of me standing in their way.

One night our gander, Gregory, woke up feeling peckish so he pecked at the leg of a burglar trying to make off with the school video recorder.

So, what with a pig running amok in the home economics department, a ewe getting legless on elderberry wine and our goat wrecking the school country fayre, we have had some highly embarrassing but hilarious times at our school. No, life is never dull.

Some of the pupils are as bad. When I first started teaching at the school in 1974 six of my fifteen pupils taking rural studies had criminal records. I was certainly thrown in at the deep end. Part of the catchment area of the school changed soon after that and nowadays most of my pupils are decent, law-abiding, hard-working youngsters. Quite a contrast to my first bunch of misfits.

Rural studies became very popular at the school, our practical outdoor facilities encouraging boys and girls to take the subject. We had started to build up our department in 1974 with materials that were second-hand, scrounged and – I suspect – sometimes purloined. In those days rural studies was called the 'Digging Department' and was for backward pupils.

In 1982 a pair of our Kerry Hill ewes won First Prize and the Kerry Hill Female Championship at the Royal Show.

The 1986 show season had been fantastic. Our sheep won a hundred and two prizes. A rival exhibitor had made a bet with me that we could not win a hundred prizes in a season. The gauntlet had been thrown down and I picked it up. Maybe it was the pints of 'Best' that egged me on but I never could resist a challenge. It was only for a fiver but it was not just the cash – honour was at stake. We travelled almost three and a half thousand miles to seventeen shows, but as we notched up one hundred prizes plus two it was well worth every mile. The *Farmer's Guardian* summed it all up with the headline 'Terry's Kerrys Achieve Ton-Up'. Amongst the one hundred and two prizes the most important to me was the First Prize and Kerry Hill Female Championship at the Royal Show because when we first won at the Royal in 1982 one of our rival exhibitors was heard to say, 'It was just luck that a bunch of school kids won it.'

As well as the twenty pedigree Kerry Hill breeding ewes we keep calves, goats, pigs, rabbits, laying hens, ducks and geese. We also have a well-stocked greenhouse, neatly laid out and landscaped ornamental gardens, vegetable gardens and an orchard.

As well as adventures, escapades, farming and gardening, my job is teaching. I am a part-time farmer, although it has been said in the past I am a part-time teacher and a full-time farmer. Not so. I enjoy teaching; it is a very rewarding job even if it is hard going some days.

I come into school early every day including holidays and Sundays, meet the volunteer pupils and with them feed and tend the livestock.

The actual school day starts at 9.05 and ends at 3.45. The first item on the agenda is registration when I sit down and call out thirty names. This takes all of five minutes. I then take my form off to assembly . . . well, I usually take them – unless something unforeseen happens like a ewe deciding to lamb or a calf needing treatment. In such cases I take myself off to tend the animals, thus incurring the wrath of the headmaster,

Mr Beech, who frowns darkly on anyone missing the ceremony.

After assembly it is the start of period one. This lasts from 9.25 until 10 o'clock if it is a single period. Some are double. There are five periods in the morning with a break after period three; after lunch there are a further three periods with a break after period seven.

My classroom is set away from the main school building, about fifty metres across the playground. It is a mobile room, timber construction, about forty years old. Not much more than a hut really. On one side the windows look out on to the playground; on the other they have a much pleasanter view on to our rural studies land. One good thing about being away from the rest of the school is that you can see visitors approaching. This can be particularly advantageous if the visitor happens to be our headmaster, as some of our extra-curricular activities can be a little question-able – chicken gutting and wreath-making to name but two. However, it is all in a good cause, raising funds for our department.

Inside the classroom the pupils sit on stools behind long oak-topped benches, also about forty years old.

I take the second- and third-year classes for one 35-minute lesson a week. After the third year rural studies becomes an option subject, each option group getting four lessons of rural studies a week.

Much of my time is spent teaching in the classroom, or on the 'chalk face' as it is sometimes called. The classes come in, sit down, get out their exercise books and pens, and then it is eyes down for the lesson.

The first part of the lesson is where I differ from

23

most teachers. Instead of saying things like, 'Right then, how far did we get with the topic last week?' or, 'Today we are going to start a new project,' I give a résumé of what farm and garden jobs have been done in the week or days since I last saw them. Many of the pupils have not set foot in the department for a whole week so I have to bring them up to date with all the news. Other pupils will, of course, have visited the department during breaks or lunchtimes, as they will have been helping before or after school. When you have plants and livestock to care for there is always something interesting going on.

I always start our lessons by reporting such things as 'We have sold our five calves to a local farmer,' or, 'One of our goats has kidded,' or 'One of our pigs is ill.' The important items are then written down by the pupils in their exercise books under the heading 'Farm and Garden Diary'. Subjects such as maths and English do not have such unpredictable events in their departments and do not require diaries.

I then go on to talk about the things we have to sell that week. It varies with the seasons, but we always have eggs and goat's milk for sale.

After my commercial I get down to the business of teaching the lesson. The scope of rural studies is vast, and among the topics I teach is soil which I tell them is a down-to-earth subject. That is always good for a few groans and catcalls.

Other topics include fertilisers, rotations, weather, plant and animal biology, farm livestock, farm crops, vegetables, flowers, greenhouse work and ecology.

Different topics are taught in different ways. I talk a

lot and explain work to the pupils; they watch demonstrations and experiments, and carry out experiments themselves. We also complete experiments outside such as learning how to milk the goats or paring the feet of the sheep. Each pupil keeps an exercise book. Sometimes they make their own notes, using books to help them in their research, at other times they copy from the blackboard or overhead projector, and sometimes I dictate notes. I also use colour slides and videos to illustrate the different topics.

I usually ask questions as I am teaching and explaining. This question-and-answer routine gets the pupils thinking, and one of my main aims in rural studies is getting my pupils to think.

Some subjects involve a lot of theory work and little practical; however, times are changing and more practical work is getting into subjects such as maths and history. When I was at school my maths teacher was not in the least practical. I remember him asking, 'If it takes one man an hour to dig a hole how long will it take three men to dig a similar hole?' My answer was, 'A lot longer because they will all stand talking.' This sort of reply was invariably treated to a derisive 'Sit down, Terry. I should have known better than to ask.' I now know how he felt because I have got one or two jokers in my pack.

In rural studies we look at things in a practical way. Our calves are weighed and measured each week, records kept, graphs drawn to show growth rate. One week we may have a calf that is ill with scours; it will probably not put on any weight that week, it could even lose some. Calves do not put on exactly the same weight each week and, of course, when we castrate our bull calves they are sure to weigh two stones lighter!

When I first started teaching in 1974 I had some real characters to contend with. Steven Wood was one of the finest class comedians I have ever taught. I have got some right ones now, mind; many witticisms have come my way during question-and-answer time. I sometimes suspect they lie awake all night thinking them up. I remember giving a lesson on fertilisers and talking about how we use chemical symbols such as N, P and K. I asked Anthony an easy question, 'What is the chemical symbol for water?'

'H_2O Sir, but when it passes through my dog the formula changes to K_9P' was his swift and witty reply.

Another incident which springs to mind was a lesson on poultry. We had brought some chickens into the classroom and I was getting the pupils to observe the birds. I asked such questions as: 'Which parts of the bird's body are not covered with feathers?' 'How many toes does the bird have on each foot?' 'Has the chicken got any ears?' The lesson was going well until I asked, 'Is the chicken warm or cold to touch?'

'Warm,' was the reply from Angela.

'What do you think the temperature of the chicken is then, Angela?' I asked.

'Do you mean when it's just come out of the freezer or at gas mark 4?' was her reply.

Another time I was giving a lesson on potato-growing to a fifth-year class and, after discussing things like varieties, planting, weed control, harvesting and storage, we went on to talk about the use of the crop. Most are sold for domestic cooking, some are sold for crisps, others are used for stock feed.

'How about potato tops, can we use them in any way?' I asked.

'I think . . .' said Helen thoughtfully, 'they are poisonous.'

'Is that correct? Are potato tops poisonous?' I asked Graham.

'Oh yes, Sir. One bite and you've had your chips.'

Camouflage was the title of a lesson to a third-year class. We looked at various means of camouflage for insects, birds and mammals.

'When Polar bears lie still they resemble a pile of snow,' said Claire.

'When Brown bears lie still what do they resemble?' was the witty reply from Simon.

I was proud to attend this school as a pupil and I am proud to have returned to teach there. The headmaster, Mr Beech, often says he wished he were head of a 'normal' school with 'normal' teachers and

'normal' pupils and no rural studies. But I always ask him what sort of a life would it be without the daily dodging of stampeding cattle, berserk pigs and marauding sheep. Would he not miss the hassle of a teacher having to drop everything to attend to sheep with stomach ache? Does he not enjoy coping with a curious goat peering through the classroom door obviously intent on joining the lesson? He usually just sniffs and replies stiffly, 'Quite so, Mr Terry.' But it is a fact that with animals and children about there is never a dull moment.

It was now time to make another decision – did we really need a dairy cow as well?

Crystal

I DID think about Carol's suggestion that we branch out into dairy farming, but it was a very busy time and I had enough farm work to cope with without taking on more. Carol and one or two of the other pupils mentioned the subject from time to time but I said not at the moment.

At the Royal Show, Carol, Diane and Stuart came for a walk around the showground with me after the sheep judging had finished, and I fell for it. They led me in a roundabout way to the cattle lines.

'A Jersey would be ideal for school,' said Stuart pointing to a very fine animal. The Jerseys certainly looked superb. I had to admit that a Jersey in our paddock would look lovely, and educationally it would bring about endless lessons. It was certainly time for a new challenge but – Jersey cattle? Could this be it?

I promised my pupils I would give it some serious thought. We chatted with a few Jersey exhibitors and I went home thinking Jerseys.

I looked at some facts and figures. I had been given a book – *The Jersey - A Guide to the Breed* – at the show and had found it most helpful. When I talked it over with some of the exhibitors we had highlighted the obstacles but I was used to those and I was definitely coming round to the idea. A calf would be fairly inexpensive to buy but she would then have to be reared on substitute milk to start with, then concentrate feed and hay. There would be a few veterinary bills to pay and she would not calve until she was two years old or over. There would be no income before she calved.

After calving she would give about four thousand litres of milk in each lactation which, if sold to the Milk Marketing Board at 18.2p a litre, would be worth £728. It probably would not be sold to the Milk Marketing Board but this figure gave me some idea as to what the milk would be worth. It would probably be fed to the pigs and so save on pig feed bills. The calf would have to be fed during the year: about 1.3 tons of concentrate feed at £150 per ton, a ton of brewer's grains at £20, plus fertiliser costs of £80. This would give a margin over all purchased feed of £513, and a margin over feed and fertiliser of £433 per cow – assuming you were selling the milk. I was not really sure what savings the milk would have on pig meal – none of my farming friends could help me out on that one either. Also we would need to buy hay and straw and pay other various miscellaneous expenses. After calving there would be a calf to sell but if it was a bull calf he would be almost worthless – of course only a few special Jersey bull calves are used for breeding purposes and they do not make popular beef animals. A heifer calf might be worth £60 or £70.

I thought of the idea of selling milk in bottles, but my pupils informed me this was a non-starter. The milk would not be pasteurised and I did not think I would be able to sell that to school children. I could not risk food poisoning or a TB epidemic, so that idea went out of the window.

Dairy farmers had been told to cut back on production, there was too much milk. Milk quotas had recently come in, so if we sold milk – or butter and cheese for that matter – I knew that we would need to purchase some quota. I thought the butter and cheese was a possibility – the milk need not be pasteurised – and I could probably collaborate with our home economics department. We could produce the milk and take it up to them; they could process the butter and cheese and package it in our own printed packets. I did not know much about yogurt or ice-cream making but perhaps even this held possibilities. I also realised that we would have to be registered with the Milk Marketing Board. Furthermore, the Ministry of Agriculture would have to give the go-ahead with our premises, and then there would be other checks on us. I remembered only too well the terrifying Miss Smart, the lady who inspected the cowshed on the farm where I had first worked, and the memory always brought me out in a cold sweat. I wondered if I would have to erect a separate building to milk the cow in or whether she could be milked in one of the existing buildings. No doubt the Ministry of Agriculture officials would soon tell me. I did not fancy the idea of milking by hand, either. A portable milking machine would be ideal, although I assumed it would be expensive. At this stage I did not know just how expensive.

So, there would be no income for the first two years. And, even after the two years, if we did not sell butter or cheese there would be no direct income apart from the possible sale of calves. However, there might be substantial savings on pig food. Our pigs lived on free out-of-date baby food, with the addition of some bought-in feed. We could increase our pig enterprise or rear calves on the Jersey's milk. Substitute calf milk was at least £20 a bag. If the cow suckled some calves we would not have to milk her ourselves. But the udder would not be the same shape with calves suckling her, and I wanted a cow with a good-shaped udder as I thought I might like to start showing.

Then, after a pause for breath, I would think again and tell myself that I was doing enough already without starting another enterprise. I waited a bit longer, thought things out very carefully and then decided on a 'Yes' vote.

My three pupils, Carol, Diane and Stuart, were over the moon when I finally gave in and said 'Yes'. Carol had shown our sheep at the top agricultural shows and sheep had been her main interest. However, she now asked me if she could give up the sheep and let someone else have a chance with them as she would like to help with the Jersey. 'After all, it was my idea, Sir,' she said.

Diane and Stuart jumped up and down for joy and asked if they could help with the Jersey too. Stuart had been helping on the school farm for some time. Diane had not been helping for long but she was proving to be of great benefit and wanted to go into an agricultural career. I agreed – the decision was made – we would buy a calf.

I told all my classes that we were going to buy a Jersey heifer calf, to keep her, milk her, breed from her and hopefully show her at local shows. Many of the pupils were enthusiastic but knew very little about Jerseys except that they were pretty cows with big brown eyes that could melt a heart of stone, and that they gave rich milk. Thank goodness I knew a bit more than that but I was interested to read anything

I could about them. I could then answer the flood of questions.

Jersey Island is considered the home of Jersey cattle. The importation of Jerseys back to Jersey Island was prohibited in 1763. They were first recorded in England in 1741 when eight cows came over from Jersey.

Jersey cattle are renowned for the quality of their milk, averaging just under four thousand kilogrammes of milk at 5.2 per cent fat and 3.8 per cent protein. This is very rich compared to Friesian milk. The fat globules in Jersey milk are large which makes the milk ideal for butter-making. The cows mature quickly and calving at two years old is common; they usually calve easily. Jersey cows are docile, very easy to handle and long-lived. They are attractive, feminine-looking cows, usually brown in colour but can be almost black or almost white. They have a dished face, a light coloured ring around their noses, and usually have black on the end of their tails. Numerically the Holstein/Friesian is the largest breed in the world; the Jersey comes second to this.

Thinking about cows reminded me of my old boss Mick who kept Friesians and did not like Jerseys one little bit. One of his farming neighbours, Cyril Webster, kept Jerseys and the arguments that ensued between these two on the merits of Friesians versus Jerseys often threatened to get out of hand although, no matter how heated the argument, they always remained the best of friends.

On a Saturday night in the Black Horse the talk between Cyril and Mick would inevitably turn to farming. Mick could talk about nothing else. Nine times out of ten the subject of Friesians versus Jerseys (sounds like a football fixture) would come up.

I was with them one Saturday when war almost broke out. I was working for Mick at the time so I dared not take sides.

'My Friesians give a lot more milk than your Jerseys do – my yields are just going up and up. They have improved so much more since the war,' bragged Mick slurping over his pint at the same time.

'Here we go again,' I thought to myself.

'The yields of my Jerseys have gone up as well. These last few years they have almost doubled,' retaliated Cyril.

'If they have doubled they must have been pretty poor a year or two back,' laughed Mick. 'They're still poor now. They can't match my Friesians.'

'No they can't – at least not for quantity. But they beat you on quality and we get more money per gallon because it's better quality,' said Cyril, getting quite red in the face.

'Yes – maybe you do but in the long run my Friesians make more profit than your Jerseys do.'

'I don't think so,' Cyril exclaimed. 'Your Friesians eat more concentrate feed and hay than my Jerseys.'

'Doesn't matter. I grow most of it myself.'

'You don't grow cattle cake,' argued Cyril. 'And if your Friesians were doing that well you would have a posh car and other luxuries in life. I don't see any of these things. . . .'

The wrangling and swigging of pints went on till well after closing time and in desperation the long-suffering barmaid declared open season on them with words to the effect that if they had not got any homes to go to she had, and if they did not remove themselves from the premises immediately she would have no qualms about sweeping them out with the fag ends.

The years rolled on and to be perfectly honest Cyril's farm was not doing very well. There was even a rumour that he might have to go into voluntary liquidation. Cyril was a determined man, however, and would not give up without a fight.

Then one Saturday night in the Black Horse they started again.

'Friesian milk is nothing but water,' snarled Cyril.

'Rubbish! Friesian milk is quite normal – but that Jersey milk is too damn rich and creamy for my liking,' retorted Mick, up in arms.

'I'll tell you what – you could place a ten pence piece on top of Jersey milk and it would stay there, the milk is almost solid but try putting it on top of Friesian milk and it will sink straight to the bottom. Not only that – if you peered over the top of the glass you would see the ten pence lying at the bottom. In fact, the milk is so watery I bet you could even read the date on it.' With that, the dozen or so men around the table all roared with laughter. Mick was furious. Mick was beaten, but only for the time being.

A couple of months later, mid January to be exact, these two characters were in the pub again.

'My muck spreader's broken down, can I borrow yours?' asked Mick.

'Course you can,' replied Cyril.

'I'll fetch it in the morning, then.'

Mick arrived early and started looking for Cyril. Cyril was still milking the cows. Mick went into the cowshed – it was the old fashioned sort – the cows being tethered by chains. As soon as he entered the shed Mick spotted it – a black and white Friesian tied up at the end of the line. It was immediately obvious to Mick that Cyril could not make the Jerseys pay and so had bought a Friesian. Mick's moment had arrived and he was going to milk it for all it was worth.

'What's this then, Cyril? Have you seen sense at last? Are you going to admit that your Jerseys don't pay?'

Cyril, however, was ready with a witty come-back.

'Well, I've been getting trouble with the water pipes freezing up so I bought the Friesian. I thought I could milk her first then if the water in the pipes does freeze up I can use her milk to wash the cows' teats with.'

A brilliant answer but in the end Cyril lost because two years later he had sold every Jersey and kept nothing but Friesians.

However, in spite of Cyril's sad story the right type of Jersey are a profitable business venture. I certainly had it in mind to make one pay and I was looking forward to making a few enquiries about buying one.

There are registered Jersey herds in Warwickshire and Leicestershire, some of them well known recognised breeders in the Jersey world. However, if I was only going to buy one Jersey I really wanted a first class animal that would hopefully give a lot of milk and would breed show stock.

I was now well experienced at breeding and showing the Kerry Hill sheep and I knew it was no good trying to breed top-quality show stock from third-rate sheep, or in other words trying to breed race horses from cart horses.

'Where are we going to buy our Jersey from?' asked Diane.

'How about the Queen, Sir?' joked Carol.

'That's a brilliant idea,' agreed Stuart.

'Let's write to the Queen at Buckingham Palace,' shouted Carol, getting quite excited and jumping up and down.

'You cannot be serious,' I said, doing a fair impression of John McEnroe.

'Yes Sir, come on let's write.'

'You write if you want to. I don't want to end up in the Tower.' I did not tell them I had had the same idea myself some months before when I first started looking at stock.

After lunch the three excited pupils, Carol, Diane and Stuart, got out their notebooks and began to plan a letter between them. I said I would leave it all to them to write, but to be honest I did read it through and corrected a spelling mistake and put in some commas. The letter asked if we could purchase a calf from the Queen. But not just any calf – a pedigree Jersey heifer from the Queen's herd at Windsor. The pupils would show the calf, get her in calf by a top bull and then hopefully show the calves that the school bred. The calf should also have the potential to be an excellent milker. It was not much to ask – was it? The letter was posted on 26th January 1987, and then my pupils eagerly awaited a reply.

Then on the 18th February the long wait was over. In the pile of school post was a letter with no stamp on it but a blue E.R. with a crown above it in a blue circle, plus a red stamp marked 'Official Paid Windsor Berks'. I collected the letter and then called the pupils together for them to open it. With a warning from me not to get their hopes raised too high, they took the letter. Excitement was rife but they opened the envelope with care and very sensibly did not snatch or tear at it. Once opened, the envelope revealed a letter from the Queen's farm manager of the Royal Farms at Windsor. He said they had no Jersey calves for sale but if we would like to be patient and possibly wait until the spring there might be a Jersey heifer calf available for us at that time. The manager said he would get back in touch with us in April. My pupils were delighted.

I told Mr Beech and various other members of staff. Some said 'Well done', others admired us for our cheek, some just confirmed in their own minds what they had suspected all along, that we were completely and utterly barmy. Mr Petty did not approve at all as he had no time for the Royal Family. Mr Beech was pleased, though, and it was reported to me by another member of staff that Mr Beech had said that he could be one step nearer his MBE or OBE. After all, he was head of the school, not Mr Terry.

My pupils were looking forward to April, and in mid-March started to count the days. We had decided that the calf would be kept in our brick buildings; these are divided into four sections. They contained four pigs, foodstuffs, three rams that we intended to show and four show ewes. We would move the rams into the wooden building and the Jersey could have their place, a section measuring seventeen by eight feet was obviously large enough for a baby calf. I also expected that she would be kept in there when she was older and even fully grown. I planned to house her during the winter but keep her out during the summer, bringing her in at night for security.

I did not at this stage need to buy any special equipment because we had been raising calves since 1974, the year I started work at the school. Our first two had been called Pinkie and Blackie; our next would have the prefix Windsor. All we could do now was wait.

When the letter arrived from the Royal Farms manager it was, to say the least, disappointing. Nearly all the newborn calves had been bulls, and there were only a few heifers. Consequently there was not a suitable heifer calf for us. It looked as if we would have to wait until the autumn when some more cows were due to calve.

Carol, Diane and Stuart were feeling as deflated as I was. I was pleased that it was lambing time, keeping us all busy so that our minds were kept off the disappointing news from Windsor. Hot on the heels of lambing we were showing again. Our sheep took priority so the Jersey enterprise was pushed into the background and was just something to look forward to.

I telephoned the Royal Farms early in October. The telephone actually rings at Windsor Castle and then you are put through to the Farm by a switchboard operator. I spoke to the farm secretary who was most helpful. She promised to remind the farm manager who would probably get something sorted out for us and then telephone back or write to me.

The days dragged by for the three pupils. At last we received a letter from the manager to say that a suitable heifer calf had been born on the 20th October. I should telephone the Royal Farms to arrange a time to visit and hopefully collect her. The letter did not mention the cost of the calf and this worried me a bit. What if it was thousands of pounds? I did not want to look a fool.

I telephoned the farm, but unfortunately the manager was out. I told the farm secretary that I could visit them at any time to suit them but Wednesday morning would be best as I had two free periods and so would need less cover for lessons from the staff. Mr Beech was very keen that I should go on a Wednesday. I thought he might ask to come with us – after all we did not know if any of the Royal Family might be there. The Royal Farm manager would telephone me to arrange details at 5pm on Tuesday.

School finishes at 3.45 in the afternoon. My pupils and I worked hard as usual feeding the livestock. I then ran up to the school office getting in there at 4.55pm.

'What can I do for you Mr Terry?' asked Mrs Loveridge, the school secretary, carrying on typing as she spoke.

'I'm expecting a telephone call from the Queen at 5pm,' I answered.

'The Queen of what?' she asked again, still not looking up from her typewriter.

'Well the Queen of England actually, but I don't suppose it will be her making the call. I expect it will be someone on her behalf.'

'You do talk a lot of rubbish sometimes, Mr Terry – the Queen of England indeed,' she said – still not looking up from her typing.

At that moment the telephone rang. She stopped typing and answered it. From where I stood I could

hear the loud, clear voice on the other end. 'Good afternoon,' the voice rang out. 'It's the Queen's farm manager here. I am calling to speak to Mr Terry concerning the purchase of one of the Queen's Jersey calves.' Mrs Loveridge's face showed all the emotions – disbelief, alarm, concern, panic, pride – all in a fleeting moment. She stood up, tidied her hair, brushed her skirt, almost saluted and bowed, got excited and knocked her pile of neatly typed letters to the floor and then she froze. Rooted to the spot, she stood open-mouthed and speechless.

'Hello. Is anybody there?' queried the voice at the other end of the line.

'Oh-er-yes, Sir,' she squeaked. 'Hold on, Mr Terry's here now.' She turned to me and said, 'It's for you.'

I suppressed a smile and took the telephone from her shaking hand.

'Is it my call from the Queen?' I grinned at her. 'Is it her personally this time or one of her representatives?' I asked casually.

'It's one of her representatives – The farm manager,' she whispered.

'Ah good. I'll take the call in the other office,' I said, even more casually.

The farm manager told me that we could visit the Royal Farm on the next day – Wednesday 4th November. He gave me directions as to how to get there. It was easy – the M1 for most of the way, then take the M25 with easy directions to Windsor and the Royal Farm. I said we would arrive at 9am. I wanted to get back to school at lunch time so that other staff would not need to cover for me in the afternoon. Mr Beech was pleased that I was going, and told me that if the Queen or any other member of the Royal Family happened to be about I should ask one of them to present the prizes at prize giving.

The three pupils who had written to the Queen – Carol, Diane and Stuart – were all very eager to come with me, so they went home and obtained letters of permission from their parents. At 5.45 the next morning they were all waiting for me even though I was on time. As on all our trips, they had come prepared with flasks of coffee and packs of sandwiches. It was a cold morning, but at least it was fine.

43

We made good time and stopped just outside Windsor for refreshments. Our directions led us straight to the farm. A gatekeeper dressed in a smart green uniform checked our identity and our line of business. He knew we were coming and had already been given the number of the car. I had given the registration to the farm manager on the telephone.

A long private drive led us to the Royal Farm. Old, strong buildings with character blended comfortably with new modern ones to make an impressive sight and as we got closer we could see that there was a place for everything and everything was in its place.

'It looks a tidy set-up,' remarked Diane.

'I suppose "she" can afford the staff to keep it tidy,' said Stuart casually.

'Yes, well just make a mental note. No shovels lying about for anyone to fall over, no rakes lying with prongs up – get my meaning?'

'Aw come on Sir, that's not fair,' they choroused. These three were quite good at putting their tools away after them, but seeing the Royal Farms looking so beautifully neat and tidy might encourage them to come down like a ton of bricks on the careless minority.

We were met by the farm herdsman, Trevor Burrwood. We introduced ourselves, and after the formalities Trevor gave us a very interesting talk about farming at Windsor. As we imagined, it is a large farming enterprise covering about twelve miles by six miles with 800 hectares which is about 2000 acres of land. The 130 pedigree Jerseys are probably the most famous enterprise but as well as these there were an Ayrshire herd, seventy large white/Landrace sows, turkeys, and an agisted flock of sheep which tidy the grassland from October to February. The arable operation is intensive with 370 hectares of winter wheat, 92 hectares of winter barley, 170 hectares of rape and 54 hectares of beans.

Royal interest dates back to Anglo-Saxon times. The farms are on mixed soils – including some very heavy clay. Much of the area is wooded and Trevor told us that they had problems with pigeons and rabbits eating the crops. The local Safari park at Windsor had provided the Royal Farms with lion dung. This had been placed around the outside of the wheat fields and had stopped the rabbits from eating the wheat because the smell of the muck frightened them. This had all the makings of a very tall story, but it turned out to be true. I wondered what novel idea they would cook up to get rid of the pigeons.

Trevor then showed us the Jersey cows. The herd was founded by Queen Victoria. They are a super herd averaging 4,400 litres of milk per cow at 5.76 per cent butterfat and 4.10 per cent protein. Their best achievement at showing was in 1982 when a pair of Windsor cows won the Burke Trophy which is the award for the champion pair of dairy cattle of any breed at the Royal Show. Over the years many of their cattle have been exported to the Middle East, Brazil, Africa, USA and Canada. Most of the cows were housed in cubicles but some were loose-housed. They are milked in a modern herringbone parlour which fits into a large grand cowshed. The dairy was created by Prince Albert, the Prince Consort, and is a very elegant affair. It has marble-top tables and exotically tiled cavity walls which are four feet thick, it even has stained-glass windows. Here cream and cream cheese are processed for the Royal Family.

When in residence at Windsor, the Queen and other members of the Royal family pay frequent visits to the farm and talk with the farm staff. The Queen's main interest on the farm is her Jersey herd and apparently she is very knowledgeable on the subject.

As was to be expected, the Jerseys really did look first class. We were shown the mother of the calf we were hoping to buy and I took some photographs of her. She was bred by the Queen and was called Windsor Banknotes Crystal. We were then shown the calves. I could feel the excitement building up in all of us. We wondered which one would be ours. They were all housed in individual pens. 'This is Crystal,' said Trevor pointing to a small two-week-old brown calf lying in the straw. 'Or Windsor Coronets Crystal 6th to give her her full title.' The name was bigger than the calf: she was so small – a cute little scrap, looking more like a fawn than a calf. There was a chorus of 'Ah, isn't she lovely' from my three pupils.

'She has an excellent pedigree. Her sire is Ferdon Glens Coronet, who sired the two Royal Show Burke Trophy winners, Windsor Coronets Blue Lily and Windsor Coronets Bunty. They are Crystal's half-sisters. You have seen the calf's mother, Windsor Banknotes Crystal. They are all bred by the Queen, so tell me – do you think the calf is good enough for you?'

'Good enough?' exclaimed Diane. 'We can't get any better than that.'

'She certainly is good enough,' I said, and Carol and Stuart agreed without hesitation. Trevor told us that the farm secretary had typed out her pedigree for us. It was a very impressive document. On the top it said Breeder – H.M. Queen Elizabeth II. Ear number HM136. It would look very prestigious on our rural studies classroom wall.

'The Queen can't give you the calf but we thought eighty pounds would be a fair price.' Eighty pounds? I could have dropped. Small cross-bred calves at our local market fetched more than eighty pounds. I did not dare haggle the price. As they say in certain commercials – that would do nicely. It was very fair. Before I visited the farm I had visions of myself and Her Majesty getting our heads together and haggling, bartering with my usual currency of course – a dozen new-laid eggs.

Trevor did not want paying there and then – the invoice would be sent to us. We all thanked Trevor very much indeed. 'You can have her for eighty pounds as long as you promise one thing – when it's time to breed with her don't take her to the nearest bull down the road at the nearest farm.'

Diane's brow furrowed 'But . . . why can't Mr Terry take her to the nearest bull down the road?' she asked in all innocence.

'Look, let me explain,' said Trevor patiently. 'It's the equivalent of Mr Terry taking Princess Anne out for the night. It's just not done.'

'Well! That's put me in my place hasn't it?' I remarked.

'You've got a good calf there. She should make an excellent milker. Crystal is capable of producing a high-yielding show calf if the right sire is used. She has excellent potential, so don't waste time getting a third- or fourth-rate bull to her. Only the best will do.'

'Will she have to come back here for her honeymoon?' asked Carol.

'No, there will be no need for that. It will be done artificially. I expect you know all about Artificial Insemination or AI.'

The three pupils did know all about it and so there was no need to explain it to them. However, many pupils back at school would need some tuition.

Trevor had shown us photographs of Crystal's relations at shows including the Burke trophy winners in 1982.

'1982 was a good year for us too. Our Kerry Hill ewes were female champions at the Royal Show.' Carol was busy telling Trevor about our triumphs with the sheep. I was delighted with this as it would prove to him that we were good with livestock and proved we would do our best with Crystal. She would be treated well – which roughly translated means spoiled rotten – and would have a good home.

I had put plenty of straw in the back of the trailer. Trevor said the whole of the trailer was too much space for the calf so we sectioned off a small area for her with straw bales. Once he was satisfied he went back into the calf building. He emerged a few minutes later with the little calf with a hessian sack tied around her middle to keep her warm on the journey. We closed the ventilation flaps on the trailer and Trevor carefully picked her up and carried her into the trailer. We put the back of the trailer up, she mooed a couple of times and then went quiet.

I had asked Trevor if we could purchase half a

bag of substitute dry powdered calf milk. I wanted to keep her on the same brand and thus avoid an upset stomach. She was used to being fed the powdered milk with three pints of warm water twice a day.

Back at school our Hereford × Friesians were getting four pints a day but they were much bigger animals. Crystal would soon start to eat solid foods and nibble hay – she was probably already doing just that.

We thanked Trevor again, got into the car and made our way back down the long drive, through Windsor and onto the motorway for the long haul back to the Midlands. We stopped after a few miles to see if Crystal was all right and then twice more before we got home. On one of our stops we took time off to finish our sandwiches. It had been a long morning and we suddenly realised we were as hungry as wolves. We made good time after that and, although we stopped three times in all, we arrived back at school towards the end of the lunch hour. I reversed the car and trailer into position and unloaded our calf. The pupils knew where we had been and I had a large audience, everyone eager to get their first glimpse of our royal calf. I let down the flap of the trailer and after a cautious look around Crystal made the grand entrance. We placed her in the clean building – she looked terrific. With her big eyes and deer-like appearance she was going to be a great favourite.

We soon noticed she was a very lively, high-spirited little lady with more fizz in her than a bottle of pop. She made our Hereford × Friesians look positively staid. She was forever running, jumping about and kicking her heels in the air. Mr Beech paid a visit the next day and other members of staff drifted across to

49

'have a look', even the ones who had declared us to be 'absolutely bonkers'. I did not want to disturb her too much in the first few days. I wanted her to settle in. She soon did this and was not timid or frightened. She was charmingly bold and came to the door for attention.

A week after her purchase I contacted various newspapers and two television crews. Andrew Jordan from Central Television, along with cameraman and sound technician, were the first to report. Andrew had filmed us before. They filmed Crystal lying down in the straw and then we turned her out on to the lawn. She loved this freedom. She had never seen so much open space and she made the most of it. She ran around – in top gear – skidded to a halt, then off she went again. Round and round getting up a bit of speed but then she came to grief, but only slightly. Cornering too fast, she knocked over a camera. Fortunately no damage was done.

The next day another television interviewer, Godfrey Brown of BBC Midlands Today, came out with a film crew. They filmed Crystal drinking from a bucket, running around the garden and then they filmed some of our other livestock. They interviewed my three pupils and asked about their letter to the Queen. It went well and my pupils did the school proud. The BBC certainly went to town – we had an excellent first-class report on the BBC Midlands Today programme. We were also on Breakfast Time and at teatime we made John Craven's News Round. These last two programmes are both screened nationwide, so I was doubly pleased.

Because the BBC had made such a good job of it

Central did not televise their efforts which was very disappointing for us. Of course all the local newspapers did a report including photographs. Then we got a telephone call from *The Times*. A photographer came the next day and worked hard all morning to get a good photograph. The one that was used showed Crystal being held up on Carol's arms (it was the only way we could get her to keep still) with an assortment of livestock in the background. Mr Beech announced in assembly next morning that we would be in *The Times* on Thursday.

Thursday morning saw at least twenty pupils troop into school with a copy of *The Times* tucked under their arms. It was an amusing and amazing sight. I suppose

in a 'normal' school with a 'normal' teacher the pupils would be perusing *The Beano* or *Jackie*, although at our school the *Sporting Life* has made more than one appearance.

Working With the Sheep

BECAUSE OF the trouble with the dogs, a local farmer friend, Matt Corbutt, agreed to keep our ewes and lambs at his farm, but only for two weeks. I therefore needed to find – and fairly quickly – somewhere to put our stock. It was nearing the end of May; we had finished lambing and could claim a very respectable total of twenty ewes and thirty-one lambs. We were well pleased but this new crisis was very worrying.

I tried my best to find grass keep at our local farms but to no avail. Most of the farmers are dairy farmers who need all their grass at that time of year either for grazing or making silage.

Richard Jonas was the most helpful of the farmers I approached. Although unable to let me have any pasture land he came up with the suggestion that I should try David and Jill Price, large arable farmers, growing wheat, barley, sugarbeet and oilseed rape. They had one small grass paddock next to the farmhouse, which was for their daughter's horses. However, their daughter had recently sold the horses and gone to college.

Richard advised me to get a move on because the grass was getting too long for sheep to eat and would soon only be suitable for hay.

So, deciding on my 'down-on-my-luck' routine, I

borrowed an old car, dressed in my scruffiest clothes and sallied forth to see what could be done.

The large farmhouse was delightful. It stood square and solid at the end of a long drive. It had an air of permanence about it. Permanence and dependability. One could imagine any farmer retreating behind its strong walls for a few hours' peace and quiet away from the rigours and stresses of farming. Make no mistake about it, farming is rigorous and stressful. It is a 365-days-a-year job. Cows do not milk themselves, sheep do not dip and shear themselves, crops do not sow themselves and grass does not eat itself. Animals become sick, and without some knowledge of animal husbandry the farmer is faced with astronomical veterinary bills. And forms? There are forms for the Ministry of this, forms for the Department of that, forms for the Office of something else. You name it and you can lay odds there is a form for it. However, this house seemed to say that no matter what else in farming changed it would stay the same, its white rendered walls defying anything that time could hurl at it.

The garden was an absolute picture – a jigsaw puzzle subject. Flowers, fruit and vegetables flourished under someone's loving hand. A fish pond lent an air of sophistication and a fence separated the garden from the field.

I knocked at the door and rang the bell but there was no answer. I was just about to walk away when suddenly Jill Price answered the door. 'What can I do for you?' she asked. She was a pretty, petite lady and very smartly dressed.

'Richard Jonas told me that you might be prepared to rent the grass paddock,' I replied.

'It's my husband David you want,' she said, and then I was conscious of a huge woolly sweater at her side. I shifted my gaze horizontally from her face and stared the woolly jumper straight in the solar plexus. My eyes travelled up and up and up and up. He was a mountain of a man, six foot six inches tall and about the same round his girth. Under the sweater was an old shirt and an enormous pair of baggy trousers held loosely round the waist by a heavy leather belt. He was a real farmer.

When you are only five foot four inches and tip the

scales at nine stones, anyone over five foot eight looks enormous. My initial reaction was that he must be Warwickshire's answer to 'Giant Haystacks' or maybe it was our local wrestling celebrity, 'Scrubber' Daly, gone into retreat.

'Hello,' he boomed in a deep, gravelly voice that emanated from that cavernous chest. 'What can I do for you?'

'I'm John Terry,' I squeaked and put on what I hoped was my friendliest smile. In hindsight it was probably more like a sickly grin. I started to explain about the school farm and our desperate search for new pasture.

'Oh really? Sounds interesting. Come on in.' I stepped inside and he listened to my tale. Then took me out and showed me the field. It was old pasture land, level, good green grass with a few trees which would be nice for the sheep to lie under in hot weather. However, it was not stock-proof.

'Richard Jonas told me you were coming so I telephoned the estate agent and asked them what I should charge. They reckon about seventy-five pounds an acre rent,' he said. He was a sharp one. We would have to indulge in a bit of serious bartering here.

'It's just what we're looking for,' I said truthfully, 'but we couldn't run to that.' After a bit of haggling I got him down to fifty pounds an acre. Half was to be paid up front and the other half to be paid in September when the sheep would be taken off the field for more grass keep which was about ten miles away. I had used this other land for a number of years now. It was a dairy farm and our sheep did the grassland good by grazing it from the middle of September until the beginning of January.

David turned out to be a very friendly person. Beneath the rough exterior and deep booming voice lurked the original gentle giant. He was a caring man with an innate love of children and animals, and it was woe-betide anyone who inflicted pain or harm on any of these innocents. Many a time I have seen David explode in anger over some news item of child or animal cruelty.

I was invited into the house for a cup of tea and I talked to Jill. Although she was the wife of an arable farmer, she liked livestock. 'We had two horses,' she said, 'but now we have nearly a thousand acres and not even a dog.'

The field was only a few miles from school, so next evening I was joined by half a dozen pupils who had cycled over for an inspection and to help make the field stock-proof.

'I don't want hundreds of unruly kids here,' shouted Jill from the downstairs living room.

I looked at the pupils and grimaced. 'Looks as if we've all got to be on our best behaviour,' I said.

I took a half-roll of wire sheep netting out of the car boot and unrolled it. It looked small and insufficient.

The house and garden were fenced off but at the side of the house was a large wood which had to be fenced off completely, requiring some fencing posts as well as wire. Around the edge of the field I would need to knock the occasional post in, but fortunately I would be able to staple into the many posts already in the hawthorn hedge. It would be quite a big job, though.

So, as with the field at Lord Clifton's, job number one – fix the fence.

'I'll go and buy the wire and posts as soon as we have measured up the field,' I stated to anyone and everyone who was listening. 'So how many rolls will we need?' I asked. I enjoy this real-life practical mathematics. I think the pupils do too because it is a rare occurrence for them to get the problems wrong. I passed them a tape measure and I held up a notepad and pen. We all got to work and measured the field – eight rolls would do the job. Our nearest stockist was only two miles away – situated on the A5. Our bank balance would be eaten into, what with fencing wire, posts and staples. However, I hoped we would be able to use the field in years to come, so it would be a long-term investment.

We spent the following weekend getting the field stock-proof. It took two days but was well worth the time as, again, it was a good practical lesson for my pupils. We worked well together as a team and were very pleased with our efforts.

The following Monday evening after school had finished we collected our lambs and their mothers from Mr Corbutts' farm and turned them out into our new, rented stock-proof field. They looked lost in the pasture of four acres. They must have thought it was Christmas. For the first time ever we had got too much grass, something unheard of for us. They would never munch their way through that lot so I seriously thought about buying in some ewes and lambs. I wanted some that we could sell in the autumn. Something commercial that would make us some money – to help pay for the wire and fencing posts.

I telephoned a few local farmers. Only one had anything to offer – Mr Arnold Rowlatt. He was never one to give anything away and wanted £110 for mule ewes with one and a half Suffolk X lambs. A mule is a cross between a Blue-Faced Leicester and a Swaledale. They are nice looking sheep, although the Kerry Hills will always have first claim on my affections.

Lambs are expressed in terms of lambing percentages. For example, if a farmer had a hundred ewes and they gave birth to two hundred lambs that is a lambing percentage of two hundred per cent. If the hundred ewes produced one hundred and fifty lambs it is a lambing percentage of one hundred and fifty per cent or one and a half lambs per ewe.

Arnold's sheep were young but really too expensive. I telephoned Mr Stone at Knighton and told him what I wanted. He had the answer – ten old Clun Forest ewes with seventeen lambs for sixty-five pounds a ewe – regardless of whether she had a single lamb or twins. I was getting twenty-seven head of stock for £650. They were old ewes and admittedly I would not get a good price for them in the autumn – probably only thirty pounds each. However, lambs would bring in forty pounds each. I worked out that the profit margin on this deal would be greater than that on Arnold's – always assuming the old ewes did not die of old age before the autumn.

Mr Stone had about 1,200 ewes on his farm so ten old ewes and seventeen lambs was obviously no real loss. He was not bothered about selling them but he was doing it to help us out, and as he had an excellent reputation I knew I would be sold healthy stock. I needed to see them before I could definitely say 'Yes'.

Ducks in Detention

I made arrangements to view them the following Saturday morning, accompanied by Jo, Michael and Carol. They had gone through the trauma of the dead lambs, so I thought it only fair that they should be involved with the happier time of purchasing new stock. We would take the trailer to Knighton because I expected to buy the sheep there and then.

We met at the school on the Saturday morning, and what a miserable wet morning it was. Rain torrented down from the heavy black clouds and silently I wondered whether this was an omen of ill fortune. We busied ourselves feeding the livestock then set off for Knighton in a deluge. By seven o'clock we were on the road en route for the farm. We arrived at Mr Stone's at half past nine by which time it had stopped raining. We parked the car and trailer in the very steep yard. A stream runs through this yard and the surrounding scenery makes a splendid setting. First on the scene to greet us were two very business-like border collies. They barked and sniffed around us all in curiosity, looked us up and down and decided we were friendly. A lot of barking, tail wagging and leaping in the air in welcome commenced. It was to a very noisy party that Mrs Stone answered the door. She beamed us a welcome. 'Come in all of you and have a cup of tea first,' she said.

It was a typical farmhouse kitchen with an Aga cooker. There were hundreds of rosettes on the walls, all won with Mr Stone's champion flock of Kerry Hill sheep. (He is one of our greatest, though friendliest, rivals.) After a cup of tea and a piece of Mrs Stone's delicious home-made cake, Mr Stone took the three pupils and me outside to look at the sheep. He had got them in one of his large buildings. They were fine – the lambs were different ages but it did not matter a bit. Some would be ready for the abattoir well before some of the others; they would be sold to my customers as whole lambs for their freezers.

We thanked Mr and Mrs Stone and journeyed home with our new acquisitions. Before turning the stock into the field we took them back to the school, unloaded them into a shed and set to work on them. We wormed them all, then dagged the ewes – this entails removing the dirty wool and muck from around the tail area. Finally we pared the ewes' feet. We then loaded them back into the trailer, took them to our field and turned them out with our pedigree Kerry Hill sheep.

While I was getting them into the field David and Jill came over to have a look.

'Good grief man. Where did you buy these from?' asked David scornfully.

'I bought them from a farmer in Wales today,' I answered.

'He must have seen you coming. They look a bit thin to me,' he replied.

'Well all right, the ewes are a bit thin, but the lambs are fine.'

'They look as if they're ready to drop dead,' he went on. 'A good meal wouldn't hurt them.'

'Oh come on now, David, you're exaggerating a bit aren't you? It's because you are used to seeing our pampered pedigree stock. These have come from the Welsh hills where they've been stocked heavier than ours on poorer pasture. Give them a month, then you'll see a difference in them,' I said confidently.

'Oh we will see a difference will we?' he said disbelievingly.

'Tell me about Clun Forests,' said Jill with real interest. 'I know about Kerry Hills, but not these.' It felt as if I were back in the classroom as I launched into my favourite topic.

'Clun sheep originate from the Clun area in Shropshire, and as you can see they have a dark brown face.'

I was in full flow when Jill interrupted. 'You're cruel!' I was taken by surprise by this unwarranted attack. Was she teasing me? I looked at her face. No! She certainly was not teasing. She was deadly serious.

'Why is that, Jill?' I asked. She continued haranguing.

'Because the farmer you bought these from has put metal tags in their ears.'

'They're only identification tags,' I said. 'They have

a number on them and the year in which the sheep was born.'

'It's bloody cruel,' she persisted. 'It must have hurt when they were put in and then the poor thing's got it stuck in its ear for the rest of its life.'

'Now hold on a minute,' I said. I had spotted a clincher to my argument. 'You have rings in your ears. Have you had your ears pierced?' She jutted her chin out defiantly. 'Yes,' was the short answer.

'Ha, you're looking a bit sheepish now, aren't you?' I replied. 'Your ears being pierced is only the same as those sheep being tagged.'

'No it's not. It's different and it's still bloody cruel,' she said, and stomped off in a huff.

Actually the lambs and ewes did well. After a week you could see a difference in the condition of the ewes. Even David had to admit it. The show season was now in full swing and we were again showing our pedigree Kerry Hill sheep. We were not doing quite as well as in the previous year but we were not disgracing ourselves either. We achieved Female Champions at Montgomeryshire and Reserve Female Champion at the Three Counties (Malvern) and The Royal.

By the end of July eight Suffolk × Clun lambs were ready for slaughter. I had secured my customers and all was arranged. I telephoned my customers a week before slaughter to keep them informed when one lady, a Mrs Ethel Smith, said she no longer wanted her order. That same evening, Carol, Michael and myself were checking the sheep when David came out to see what we were doing.

'Can we sell you a lamb for your freezer?' asked Carol, so completely out of the blue that for a minute even I was stricken speechless. Before David could answer she added, 'We have got eight of these lambs ready and Mr Terry found eight customers for them. But he has been let down by one customer who now says she doesn't want it.'

'It's a lovely lamb,' added Michael.

David – outnumbered – looked at me and said, 'Is this young lady your sales manager?'

'No,' I replied, having recovered the power of speech. 'But she had a good teacher.'

'Why isn't the teacher buying a lamb, then?' he asked.

'The teacher *is* buying a lamb,' I replied.

'What will a lamb cost me?' David was getting interested.

'Well, I called half a dozen freezer centres and the average price is eighty pence a pound.'

'That sounds all right. I'll have it. When will it be ready?'

'Wednesday. I'll deliver it about five in the afternoon.'

'Well done Carol,' I said as David disappeared back into the farmyard. 'I'll make a sales person of you yet.'

'I did my bit too,' said Michael.

'It was a bit as well,' said Carol sarcastically.

If a day goes by when these two do not take a stab at each other I shall be sorely tempted to call in a doctor because it will be a sure sign that one or both of them is under the weather – bubonic plague at the very least I should think.

Working with the Sheep

I took the lambs to the abattoir early Monday morning before school started. I prefer to do it at this time of day. A couple of pupils will come in and help load up. Then I will be back at school – job done – before the rest of the school arrives, so the pupils do not see the animals go. Oh yes, my lot may pretend to be hardbitten and cynical but I have had my fair share of 'scenes' to contend with on more than one of these occasions.

I telephoned the abattoir on Wednesday lunchtime. They said I could fetch the eight lambs, which would be cut up into joints and chops, after four o'clock that day.

I delivered David and Jill's lamb at five in the afternoon as promised. They were both out but their daughter, Fiona, was home from college. She explained that their freezer had broken down and that her parents had gone out to buy a new one. It was a hot, sunny day so I left the plastic bag containing the lamb on the concrete floor of a large barn, where I thought it would be cool. It was then I noticed that there was a hole in the bottom corner of the bag where a piece of bone had punctured it. Some blood had trickled out; it was nothing much so I did not mention it. It would not matter because the meat would soon be in the new freezer.

At six-thirty I telephoned to see if David had bought a new freezer and if he was pleased with the lamb.

'No, I didn't get one,' he said. 'I couldn't find one at the right price. They were all far too expensive. I shall have to look out for a second-hand one.' I smiled to myself. This was a farmer who owned a thousand acres of land plus thousands of pounds worth of buildings and machinery. Then – I panicked.

'Wait a minute. What are you going to do with your lamb? It will go bad if you leave it lying around in that plastic bag,' I was really concerned. Firstly, I did not want a perfect lamb to 'go off'. Secondly, he had not paid me for it; if it did go bad he might be loth to do so.

'Oh don't worry. The lamb will be all right,' he replied.

'Have you put it in someone else's freezer then?' I asked.

'No,' he said blithely. 'I tied the top of the bag with string and put it in the fish pond. The meat will keep cool in there and certainly won't go off.'

I swallowed the urge to scream. Instead I kept a quiet but very unsteady voice and said, 'You are joking – aren't you David?'

'No. I'm not joking. It stands to reason. The pond is in the shade, the water stays cool. So why not? The meat won't go bad in there.'

'I'm taking no responsibility – that lamb was perfect when I delivered it, so I shall want paying for it.'

'All right, don't get het up. You'll get your money. The lamb will be fine. Stop your silly worrying. You'll give yourself a heart attack.'

I just dared not say any more. I knew the bag had a hole in it and I was imagining it filling with pond weed, algae and all sorts of pond creatures such as water boatmen, daphnia, and of course the occasional goldfish going for a lookaround. David broke the silence.

'Hello John? Are you still there? John? What's the matter? You've gone awfully quiet!'

'David – what a daft idea,' I said eventually. 'Suppose the bag gets punctured and the pond water gets in.'

'It won't. It's going to be all right I tell you. The bag won't get punctured. There's nothing in the pond to puncture it.'

'I wouldn't be so sure,' I said nervously.

'Look, if the bag does get punctured and the pond water gets in we'll have the lamb for dinner and the frogs legs for "afters". Our Jill's always fancied her chances at the French cuisine,' and he roared with laughter. 'Tell you what – we could have home-made fish and chips – goldfish and chips,' and off he went again.

'I tell you David, I accept no responsibility whatsoever.'

I spent the rest of that evening worrying myself sick over that lamb. The next day, in my lunch hour, I made a quick trip over to David's house. Hoping against hope that everyone would be out, I crept into the garden and went to have a look in the pond. There was a large black plastic bag in the water. It crossed my mind that I might look highly suspicious, skulking around the garden and peering into the fish pond at a large black plastic bag. To the casual observer it could look as if David and I had conspired in murder and were hiding a body until a more opportune moment. But back to reality, it was quite obvious David had spotted the leak in the original bag and put this larger bag over it. It was a good tough bag so I assumed the lamb was all right. Of course he would not tell me this, he would just let me sweat it out.

That evening David telephoned me. My heart sank

– like that lamb, I imagine.

'I thought I'd just put your mind at ease,' he said. 'I bought a new freezer today and we have just finished packing the lamb inside. It's fine. No frogs, no beetles, nothing.'

'That's a relief,' I said. 'Glad you got a bargain – you had me worried. I worked hard producing that lamb, then I thought you were going to spoil it. I hate waste.'

'You worry too much, that's your trouble,' he said.

'I suppose I do,' I replied. But a worrier is a worrier, and I knew there was a hole in the plastic bag.

David and Jill were keen to watch the sheep. Jill would call them to the garden gate and feed them bread, cabbage leaves and other culinary delights. All of John Stone's old Clun ewes had a number sprayed on their sides and their lambs had the same number on their sides. In a big flock this is a good idea as it helps the shepherd sort them out. We do not bother to spray our sheep because we only have a few so we remember which lamb belongs to which ewe.

'How much do you want for one Clun ewe and her lamb?' asked Jill one day.

'What do you want to know for? And what do you know about sheep?' asked David sharply before I could get a word in edgeways, 'This is an arable farm,' he said sternly, not a stock farm.'

'I know nothing about sheep,' admitted Jill, 'but I bet John and his pupils would help me.' I saw David give her a sidelong look and the dread on his face at what was coming next.

'Well I can honestly say the best Clun ewe is this

one.' I pointed to her. 'The others are old but she is only three. I would want sixty pounds for her and thirty pounds for the ewe lamb.'

'That's great – I'll take them.' That was the quickest deal I have ever struck.

'You chump,' said David in disgust, 'You should have got the price down. John would have taken less money for them. Why didn't you barter with him?'

Jill shrugged her shoulders. 'Never thought about it.'

'I wouldn't have budged,' I said. 'That was my price. Take it or leave it.'

'Well it's done now,' said Jill. 'I am now the proud owner of one ewe and one ewe lamb.'

'We started with two sheep and look at us now. Our flock gets bigger every season,' I said.

She eyed our flock with a little apprehension. 'I don't want any more,' she declared with slight alarm in her voice.

'Well you can't keep them as pets,' said David. 'They'll have to be served and have lambs of their own.'

'Oh.' Doubt in the voice this time. 'Well – yes I suppose you're right really. Still – we've got plenty of room.' The old optimism was returning.

'And another thing.' David was determined to be the damp squib. 'What are you going to do with all the ram lambs you breed?'

Jill pulled a face. 'I'm not too keen on them going for meat' she said. 'Couldn't we sell them for breeding stock?'

My turn now. 'I'm afraid not, Jill. They're not pure-bred. No farmer would want to breed from them.'

69

Jill's face clouded a little at that. Then, ever the optimist, she smiled and said brightly, 'Oh well, that's a long way off. I'll cross that bridge when I come to it.'

'Oh you will eh?' said David. 'I've heard you talk before, lady.'

My pupils, Carol, Michael and Jo, had been standing on the sidelines while all this was going on but they were taking it all in. I could tell by their faces that 'Sir' was in trouble. When David and Jill were out of earshot Carol launched into the assault. 'You shouldn't have sold the ewe and her lamb to Jill. She was impulse buying. She doesn't know a thing about sheep and she hasn't thought it out, you know.'

'Carol's right, Sir,' said Michael.

'I agree with them,' said Jo. 'You shouldn't have done it.' Dissension in the ranks. One thing about these three – if they have got something on their minds they certainly believe in clearing the air.

I conceded the point. 'You're right, of course. She took me by surprise.'

'That's no excuse,' said Carol. 'You've told us enough times.' She was right again. Any class that comes under my tuition gets the standard lecture on the impulse buying of animals. And here was I indulging in a bit of selling.

'Look, it's not as bad as you're making it out to be,' I said in self-defence. 'The sheep are not going to outsiders. They're staying with our flock so we can keep an eye on them and teach Jill the rights and wrongs of sheep rearing. She's got a lot to learn – worming, dagging, lambing. You all know well enough how much there is to know. If we give her first-hand tuition

70

it will give her more incentive to look after the sheep and she will be looking at our flock as well. In the long run everyone will benefit. Besides, I haven't had the cheque from them yet so she might change her mind. Don't forget her husband – he's an arable farmer now, but he used to keep stock,' I said.

'She won't change her mind,' said Carol. 'She's too enthusiastic.'

'Well there you are then,' I said. 'You're arguing against your own case.'

And so, in the best traditions of Western films we walked off into the sunset, arguing like fury.

The Rabbit Fancier

I HAD kept rabbits as a boy, showing them at local fur and feather shows, and then when I started teaching I continued my tradition by keeping them at school. In the rural studies department we had the New Zealand Whites, which are usually kept for meat production as the adults average four kilos in weight. It is a good white meat with not much fat and is very tasty. My original idea back in 1974 had been to breed them, sell the young as pets and dispose of any surplus as rabbit meat. However, in practice, my pupils were never very keen on selling them for meat, so the surplus were all sold as pets; in fact we never killed any for meat.

I was getting bored with keeping just white rabbits and so it was time for a change. I had kept Dutch and English rabbits as a boy and they were still my favourites; both breeds have very distinctive markings. Dutch rabbits are fairly small, weighing two and a quarter kilos. There is a V-shaped white blaze down the front of the face, the V coming to a point at the front of the ears. Dark markings on the sides of the V extend to the rest of the head, and the ears are dark. The front half of the body is white, including white legs and white feet. The back half of the body is dark but with white feet. Where the white meets the dark there is a very clear line which is unbroken. Dutch rabbits can be of many different colours including black, grey, tortoiseshell and chocolate.

The English rabbit is slightly larger than the Dutch, and has a white body. Around its nose are dark markings – either black, blue, grey, chocolate or tortoiseshell – which look like the spread wings of a butterfly; in fact, the mark is called a 'butterfly smut'. The ears are dark and there is a dark patch around each eye. A dark line – which should be unbroken – runs from behind the ears to the tail which sits above the backbone. Spots (called chain spots) run in a line down each side of the rabbit; these should be evenly balanced on each side. The spots start small behind the ears and get larger towards the loins. These markings are very important if you want to show your rabbit. However it is a very difficult task to breed a really good English rabbit, although the aim of the fancier is of course to produce the perfect specimen. Well-marked ones are usually mated to partners with not many markings, known as 'Charlies'. It is a fact that this mating gives better marked specimens than mating two first-class rabbits. The English rabbit also produces a good carcass, but this would not interest us.

Ducks in Detention

I had been a member of our local fur and feather fanciers association when I was a boy, but over the years I had lost contact with them. I now got in touch with them again and explained to Bill, the secretary, that I wanted a change from New Zealand Whites. Bill gave me half a dozen addresses and telephone numbers of leading national breeders of Dutch and English rabbits. I always say it is better to buy the best stock possible – perhaps buying two or three really good rabbits rather than ten or twelve second- or third-rate specimens. In fact, one of our pupils, Gillian, asked me if the Queen kept Dutch or English rabbits, and suggested that if she did we should buy some off her, to go with our calf.

Our New Zealand White stock had dwindled to just a buck and a doe, two handsome rabbits which I sold for two pounds each to one of my keen third-year pupils. That left our hutches empty. They are good, sound, and constructed like a block of flats, three tiers high and three feet long.

Two second-year pupils were interested in rabbits: Gillian was a neat, clean, tidy girl, blonde and round faced; Ian was a small boy, quite pale and frail looking, very thin but a good, hard worker. These two thoroughly enjoyed their rural studies lessons and had asked if they could get actively involved with some work after school.

Gillian wanted a pet rabbit of her own but her parents would not hear of it and, after numerous arguments and pleas, she had still not won them over to the idea. So she compromised and agreed to help look after the school's new rabbits.

Ian was nervous and a little frightened of the larger

74

farm animals, but he liked the rabbits. I thought that perhaps they would give him more confidence and later on he could get involved with the larger stock – this has happened on many occasions with other pupils.

So, we cleaned out the hutches and manoeuvred them outside, then Gillian and Ian had a field day scrubbing them out. They sloshed the water about, scrubbed the hutches and disinfected every corner, nook and cranny, before leaving them to dry in the sun.

Gillian and Ian had visited the school library and the town library and read about rabbits, but we were still unsure which breed to keep. It was Gillian who decided. 'The English rabbits have got faces like Kerry Hill sheep – look at the photograph in this book' Ian and I both looked; I had never thought of comparing them with Kerry Hill sheep before.

'She's right, Sir. Look, they have got white faces with a black patch around their nose, black patches around their eyes and black ears,' observed Ian looking carefully at the colour photograph of a splendid exhibition rabbit in Gillian's book. 'Let's have the English breed, please Sir,' begged Ian.

'Would you like a different colour? A change from black and white?' I asked.

The two youngsters looked thoughtful. 'We could buy the grey-and-white or tortoiseshell-and-white, for instance,' I continued.

'No Sir,' they both said. 'Let's go for the black-and-white ones like our sheep,' added Gillian.

'But we have got sheep with black and white faces, black-and-white Hereford × Friesian calves, black-and-white British Alpine goats – surely enough black and white is enough,' I said.

'No Sir – we have decided we would like the black-and-white English rabbits, please,' said Ian. Gillian agreed and then so did I.

We looked down our list of names and addresses, which included three for English rabbits. I telephoned all three. Mr Davies from North Wales did not have any stock to sell, Mr Russell had, and so had Mr Jenkins. Mr Russell lived in Northumberland, but as Mr Jenkins lived on the outskirts of Birmingham, only twenty miles away, he was the obvious choice. I had a long conversation with Mr Jenkins – he was putting on his best Birmingham accent I was sure. He kept about fifty breeding does, exhibiting all over the country and was famous in English rabbit circles. I told him that we had always kept rabbits but we wanted to change our breed to English. He said that a buck and a doe that would be good enough to compete at local shows would only cost us four pounds each. It was good to be buying something that would not get us into debt, or require saving up for. We had the hutches, water bowls and food bowls, so we were ready for the newcomers.

I wanted stock that was good enough for shows, but whether we would ever get around to showing was another question. Not only were we attending about fifteen shows a year with the sheep, we were also hoping to start showing our Jersey calf, Crystal. In the showing world it is best to show just one breed of one animal, concentrate your efforts and hopefully reach and stay at the top.

If Gillian and Ian – or any other pupils – became

really interested, I might be persuaded to encourage them even more by taking the rabbits and the pupils to a local show. I would have to see how much interest we had.

It was four weeks before the end of summer term. Life was supposed to be easier now that the fifth years had left school (previously I had been teaching them for eight periods a week – the equivalent of a day). However, in practice, life was just as busy because I was invigilating for the GCSE examinations, attending many meetings organised by the headmaster, marking projects, attending parents' evenings and, of course, preparing sheep for shows.

I telephoned Mr Jenkins again and we tried to find a time when we were both free. I was busy every evening that week, but my pupils had worked hard cleaning out the hutches and I did not want to keep them waiting. I liked the idea of buying the rabbits before school. I thought it would take us about forty minutes to get to Mr Jenkins' house and, say, half an hour to look at, choose, and buy the rabbits, and then forty minutes to travel back to school. I suggested to Mr Jenkins that I would be with him at 7.30 am.

'I have never known anyone buy rabbits at that hour', he exclaimed.

'Will I get you out of bed, being so early?' I asked.

'No,' he replied very loudly and confidently. 'I will have been up for hours.'

'Can you give me some directions please?' I asked. He did – but I needed a degree in geography to follow them. I wrote them down as carefully as I could and confirmed that I would be with him at 7.30 on Tuesday morning.

Gillian and Ian were eager to come along with me, and I thought the early start would do them good. If they were going to show the rabbits, they would have to get used to early starts, and it was possible that in a few years time they would be showing sheep with me – that meant a 4.30 am start for one show.

I met them at the school gates at a quarter to seven. It was a warm morning with not a cloud in the sky. It promised to be a beautiful day. It was a very easy journey – until the last couple of miles.

Mr Jenkins' directions proved to be about as useful as a fork in a soup bowl. Diabolical was an apt description. I followed his directions and got well and truly lost. The old music hall tune 'Oh Mr Porter' drifted into my mind and I found myself singing to myself, 'Oh Mr Jenkins, what shall I do, I wanted to go to Birmingham and I am on the road to Crewe.'

Grenville Road was our destination, but could we find it? All the areas seemed to look the same, row upon row of terraced houses with no front gardens. Eventually I gave up and stopped to ask a passer-by, a gentleman walking his dog. Nine times out of ten such people are locals and know every inch of the area, but not this time. 'Never heard of it,' was his reply.

I then leaned out of the window and asked a lady walking by on the other side of the road. She totally ignored me, much to my pupils' amusement. I could see them smiling through the rear mirror.

Not to be beaten, I travelled further and asked two men who were approaching the bus stop. One was very talkative and gave me far too many directions, so I could not possibly remember everything he said. I remembered the first few directions and then asked again – a lady this time. She was very helpful, her directions were clear and I soon found Grenville Road. Cars were parked outside the houses on both sides of the road. However, there was an empty space outside what proved to be No 97 – the Jenkins house. I was able to park right outside the door. It was exactly 7.30 am.

Some of the houses looked quite bright and cheerful, but oh dear me, not this one. To say it looked shabby is being charitable. Gillian and Ian clambered out of the car, treading carefully to avoid newspapers and cans thrown carelessly down on the ground. The litter was dreadful.

The house itself was a shambles – the woodwork at some time past had been painted yellow but there was little left of it; it was probably last painted in the 1950s, I thought. I could also see that the window frames were rotten. The windows were thick with muck, and, from what we could see, the curtains were filthy. I bet the windows had not seen a leather or cleaner since the Coronation.

I sensed that Gillian was about to say something but before she could, I said, 'Don't judge a book by its cover.' Gillian had been brought up in a super house and her mother was very houseproud – this was the reason for Gillian not being allowed to have a pet rabbit. Pets would make the place untidy. Her father was a company director. They had three up-market cars and a swimming pool. I hoped Gillian would not say something rude and let me down. I knew Ian would not – he probably would not notice if the place was a hovel or a stately home. If he did notice it would not matter to him. He was a nice quiet lad.

The front door looked most uninviting. The pane of glass was missing at the top and the large gaping hole had been boarded up with exterior plywood which looked rather weatherbeaten, as though it had been there for some time. There was no doorbell, so I decided to go to the back of the house. I walked down the entry way – a covered walkway between the houses – and through the large wooden gate on the left at the top of the entry and into the back yard. My two pupils followed me obediently like two little terrier dogs.

We stopped dead in our tracks and looked around in dismay. The garden was a mess – long grass, thistles and docks thrived in abundance; there were two or three children's bicycles left out to rust, an old

80

doll's pram lay upturned and the crowning glory to all this was an old sideboard, which had weathered more than one turn of the seasons judging by its colour and condition.

I knocked on the door and waited. A dog barked. I could smell bacon. I could see by the way Gillian's nose twitched that she could too. Oh, it did smell good!

We did not wait for many seconds before a large, well-built woman opened the door. She had on a blue-and-white apron and was wearing a perfume called 'stale cooking fat'. In one hand she was holding a barking, struggling bull terrier by the collar. She had a very red round face. She took the cigarette from her mouth and yelled, 'Shut up Butch.' The dog went quiet.

'Hello, what do you want?' she asked.

'We have come to look at, and hopefully buy, some rabbits off your husband,' I said.

'At this flaming time in the morning?' she asked incredulously.

'Yes.'

'Well, he never said anything to me about it. I didn't know you were coming.'

'Oh dear,' was all I could muster.

'Come in – don't stand out there – he's not up yet – he never gets up before a quarter to eight.'

We walked in and stood just inside the door. Looking around, my worst fears were confirmed. The place was a tip. Well – it made a landfill sight look respectable. The woman walked over to the cooker. The frying pan was filled with bacon and the same delicious smell that wafted out to us on the morning air filled the kitchen, but the sight of the place put me right off. What a state it was in. Cobwebs like Nottingham lace hung in two of the corners. The once white ceiling was now yellow with age and nicotine fumes. There was no shade on the light and no mat on the floor. I am no snob but good grief, there is a limit. And Lord knows what Gillian thought.

'My name's Rose,' she said, 'and that's Grandad sitting in the corner.' I had not noticed Grandad – his plain brown suit blended in well with the chair and walls.

'I'm John Terry and these are my pupils, Gillian and Ian. My two protégés said 'Hello' very politely to both Rose and Grandad.

'Oh, I forgot to introduce you to Butch,' she said. 'He won't hurt you – he's as daft as a brush. All bark and no bite.'

I was not prepared to take that statement at face value. I had noticed his teeth when we came in. Butch had settled down in his basket and lay watching us. Probably sizing up which of these three bags of bones was going to be his dinner. He was an ugly dog – a dirty greyish white with brown markings. He had sturdy shoulders and a thickset neck. It was easy to see why the breed was used for fighting. If any budding film producer considers a re-make of *Oliver Twist* they need look no further than Butch to play Bill Sykes' dog.

Rose placed the cigarette back in her mouth and then dished the bacon out on a plate. She put the plate under the grill to keep warm and then cracked four eggs into the pan. Some cigarette ash also fell into the pan although Rose appeared not to notice. Behind the cooker the tiles were cracked and covered with grease. It was so thick you could have etched your name in it.

I looked closer at Grandad, sitting in his old rocking chair, and I saw the teapot in his lap. 'Funny sort of hot water bottle,' I thought.

'I'll give Bob a call in a minute, love,' said Rose, slopping fat and fag ash over the eggs to cook them.

'Go and wait in the living room' she said. We started to move when Grandad gave a chesty cough that sounded like a footballer's rattle and blew down the teapot spout. 'It's blocked up with tea leaves' he said and, giving an action replay of the cough, blew down the spout again.

'Do you fancy a cup of tea, love?' asked Rose generously.

'Not for me, thank you,' I replied politely.

'How about you two?' asked Rose. I fervently hoped that Gillian would not turn her nose up.

'No thank you,' they both replied. I gave a sigh of relief. Gillian had not looked down her nose.

'Get up, you lazy beggar,' Rose shouted up the stairs which led through a door directly off from the living room. There was no reply. I wondered how long we would have to wait. Time was getting on and we had to be back at school for registration at five past nine – I did not want to upset Mr Beech again.

Rose must have realised my agitation 'Don't worry, love. He's awake. He heard me but he's cocking a deaf ear. Sit down and take the weight off your feet.'

Sit down? Where? The room was cluttered with junk

and there were piles of newspapers and cardboard boxes on most of the chairs.

Suddenly there was a dull thud overhead. All three of us gazed up at the ceiling with our mouths slightly open – Mr Jenkins had obviously got out of bed. Minutes later footsteps came clumping down the stairs, the door opened and in came a boy of about fourteen. What a sight he was! With his short cropped hair, torn denims and sweatshirt, gold earring and Doc Marten boots, he was every inch a football hooligan. He looked shocked to see us sitting there.

'Morning,' I said.

'What the bloo . . .' He just stopped himself in time.

'You frightened the life out of me. I didn't expect to see anyone sitting in our living room this early in the morning.'

'Sorry,' I replied.

'Come and get your breakfast, Wayne,' shouted Rose from the kitchen. He did not need second bidding, he was off. Making straight for the door he made it obvious he did not want to make conversation with us. Gillian and Ian were very quiet. They had hardly said a word since we entered the house.

A rasping cough emanated from the upper regions. Mr Jenkins was on the move. Within seconds heavy footsteps thumped down the stairs. This was him alright. The door opened a second time and in walked an enormous man. Almost bald and wearing a string vest with more holes in it than a trawlerman's net (a good many of them made after the initial manufacturing process) and with an outsize pair of baggy trousers, he made an imposing sight. The trousers were held precariously in place by a thick leather belt and over this hung an economy-size beer belly. It must have cost him a small fortune to get it.

'I can't speak to you yet,' was his first remark.

'Oh,' was all I could say. Gillian and Ian looked at me, bewildered.

'I can't speak till I've had a fag, and then I'll be with you,' he explained. 'Got any fags?' he shouted at the top of his voice to Rose, who by this time was dishing up the breakfast (fag ash and all), to Grandad and Wayne. Rose treated him to a taste of his own medicine by 'cocking a deaf ear'. He disappeared into the kitchen and came back a few minutes later clutching the much sought after 'fag' in his hand.

It appeared that Mr Jenkins' breakfast was a cup of tea and a cough because he went off into a really good coughing session. The rasping cough we had heard earlier was just a practice run for the main bout now taking place. He was rattling worse than Grandad and bringing phlegm up from the back of his throat. I thought his heart was going to give out. At last he quietened down a bit, smiled and said, 'Ah, that's better. Now then, you are Mr Terry and these are your children.'

'Yes,' I replied. 'But these are my pupils, they are not really my children. That's Gillian and that's Ian.' I introduced them.

'Call me Bob,' he said congenially.

'He's not our Dad,' said Ian, and Gillian agreed with him.

'I expect that's your car out there is it?' he said peering out of the window.

'Yes it is,' I replied.

85

'Let's go and see my rabbits then – I won't over-charge you. I thought five pounds each,' he said, walking towards the door.

'You said four pounds each on the telephone,' I protested, not wanting to be done.

'I didn't know you could afford a car like that,' he said, pointing to my pride and joy.

'It's not that good,' I argued.

'It's a bloody sight better than mine because I haven't got one.'

We followed him through the kitchen.

'Have your breakfast before you go down to the rabbits,' ordered Rose.

'We won't have time,' was his answer, which I was very pleased to hear. We were getting short of time. Five past nine was not that far in the future now.

'Do you know, Mr Terry,' said Rose. 'I'm sure he thinks more of those rabbits than he does of me.'

'Really?' was my polite answer.

'They don't answer back,' muttered Bob.

'Don't stand in the dog muck,' cried Rose, startling Ian who was about to put one foot in a pile situated by the door. Grandad and Wayne were busy eating their breakfast and did not appear to notice the mess but it would have put me right off my food. My stomach turned over at the very thought.

Bob led us out of the door. The house was such a complete and utter shambles that I was glad to be out of it. So too, I imagined, were Gillian and Ian. I dreaded to think what state the poor rabbits would be living in. I expected the hutches to be filthy.

The garden was a jungle. I had half-expected Bob to issue us with machetes to hack our way through.

The Rabbit Fancier

I wondered if we would meet the three Davids –
Attenborough, Bellamy and Livingstone – coming out.
Fortunately there was a well-worn path leading to a
black and white shed, right at the bottom of the garden.
It was a large shed about thirty feet long by twelve feet
wide, and very smartly painted. Bob took out a key
from his pocket, opened the door and ushered us
in first.

It was a real eye opener – a shock to us all. After
coming out of that house and through the jungle we
were greeted by this sight. It was immaculate!

Each side of the shed was stacked three high with
rabbit hutches, each hutch was about three feet long,
wooden construction, with hinged doors and weldmesh fronts. Each was numbered 1–81. They were all
so well made and very, very clean. The larger floor
space in the middle of the shed was taken up by plastic
dustbins with lids on, every one clearly labelled, with
different rabbit foods. There were bales of hay and
straw and two large tables. On one table was an
electric kettle, a jar of coffee and sugar. This shed was
definitely Bob's bolt hole. His own little hide-away
to which he could retreat away from the stresses of
family life. I reckoned he spent more time in the shed
than in the house. I half-expected to see his bed in the
shed, and yes, I believed his wife when she said he
thought more of the rabbits than he did of her. The
floor of the shed was obviously swept every day, and
when I looked closer at the hutches I could see they
really were very clean indeed. The rabbits looked in
superb condition and seemed quite content in their
little 'flats'.

There were does on their own, does that were

expecting litters, does with litters, and in other hutches young stock were growing. One block of hutches was devoted to housing the bucks.

'This set-up is marvellous,' gasped Gillian in admiration.

'It really is first class,' I agreed, looking towards the ceiling for the Louis XIV crystal chandeliers. As I was talking, Bob picked up a dustpan and brush and started to clean out one of the hutches, talking gently all the while to its resident. He was like a really houseproud lady – a bit like Gillian's mother.

'I built all the hutches myself,' he said with justifiable pride, 'and I built the shed as well.'

'I expect Wayne helped you,' I said.

'Not on your life, mate. He's bloody useless. Well, not quite, you can always use him as a bad example; but that's about all he is good for.'

'I can't believe how tidy and well organised it all is,' I said. Gillian and Ian were eagerly looking at the young rabbits in the hutches. Bob had all the colours. Blacks, blues, greys, chocolates and tortoiseshells, many of them had come to the front of the hutches, curious to see who had arrived.

'They are lovely. Which can we buy?' asked Ian.

'Wait a minute and I'll show you which ones you can choose from,' said Bob. 'But look at my records first.'

He opened a drawer underneath the table and brought out a large hardbacked book – he was eager to show me – like a schoolboy awaiting my approval of his latest project. He opened it and there in exceptionally neat handwriting he showed me how he recorded which does went to which buck, the date the does gave birth, number in the litter, number reared, date of weaning and show results from some of the young. It looked so meticulous and so out of character.

'It was the black-and-white rabbits you wanted – wasn't it?'

'Yes please,' I replied.

He looked at his book, then approached cage number 19 and took out five young. He took out four more from cage 21 and five more from cage 27. They were all black-and-white English rabbits.

Gillian was not concentrating. She was looking at some young tortoiseshell rabbits. 'Couldn't we have one of these and mate it with a black and white one?' she asked.

'I'm not sure,' I replied, looking at Bob for a knowledgeable reply.

'No,' he replied. 'You don't cross a black with a tortoiseshell. You mate blacks to blacks and tortoiseshell to tortoiseshell – so which colour do you want?'

'We will go for the blacks, as agreed,' I said.

Gillian said goodbye to her new little friends and came back to see what was on the table. Bob was turning them upside down to sex them. He put the bucks on one side of the table and the does on the other.

'That buck looks good,' observed Ian.

Bob picked up the buck and placed him in the centre of the table. This rabbit's chain spots down either side were very evenly balanced.

'It's certainly a good one. It's the best one I've got to sell – you have a good eye for a rabbit, young man,' he said approvingly to Ian.

'We will have that one,' I decided.

'I'll be honest with you though. I have got one or

two better ones.' Bob turned around, took a large buck out of a cage and placed him on the table. 'This is my very best rabbit,' he said proudly. 'It's the father of the one you just picked out and he's won prizes all over the country!' My two pupils stroked the adult buck on the nose.

Then Bob picked out a sweet little doe and placed her in the centre of the table. 'I would like you to have this doe to go with the young buck. She has fewer markings than the others and is called a ''Charlie''.'

'Yes, we know about Charlies,' said Gillian.

'I thought you would,' said Bob.

'Yes, Ian's a proper Charlie,' she giggled.

'That's it then. Those two will do nicely for us.' I said.

'I'll go and fetch the boxes from the car, shall I?' offered Gillian.

'Yes please,' I said, and handed her the car keys.

'Don't get driving off in Mr Terry's car,' teased Bob.

'I won't,' she laughed. She soon returned, and we put one rabbit in each box.

'This is a lovely doe,' said Bob pointing to another young rabbit on the table. 'It's beautifully marked and would probably do well at local shows. I tell you what, have that one for four pounds, mate her with that buck you have just bought – and if the young don't turn out very well marked bring her back and mate her with another one of my bucks.'

I readily agreed and Ian popped her in the box with the other doe. I paid Bob. We were now the proud owners of three rabbits.

We took one last look at Bob's superb stock, before

The Rabbit Fancier

making our way out through the jungle, Ian carrying one box and Gillian the other.

Bob opened the door to go back in the house. I shouted cheerio to the family, but before I got an answer Rose came outside to remonstrate with Bob.

'Where have you been until this time?' Before he could answer, she continued, 'Your breakfast is ruined.' The tirade went on: 'You spend all your time with those rabbits – you are totally selfish, you don't care about your family.' I stood there waiting to go. It was embarrassing to be standing there listening to a family squabble, one-sided as it was – Bob could not get a word in edgeways. I just wanted to thank Bob again and get on my way, but Rose had another go at him.

'When was the last time you took us out? Come on, when – and I don't mean to a bloody rabbit show, either. Come on, when?' He was about to answer but she went on: 'When was the last time you took me out, I asked you. You can't remember can you?'

'I took you to see ''Sound of Music'' didn't I?' he replied.

With these words we said cheerio again and crept off down the entry way before she could set on us. I could still hear her out in the street.

'We saw ''Sound of Music'' in 1972. It's now 1988,' she nagged.

He countered with: 'I'm going to work this morning, you can come with me if you want to.'

We put the rabbits in the car and set off for school. Gillian and Ian soon started gossiping.

'His house was a tip – but the rabbit shed was like a palace,' said Gillian excitedly.

'You noticed,' said Ian sarcastically.

'The place was like a pigsty,' said Gillian.

'I beg your very pardon, Miss Posh. Our pigsties are like stately homes,' replied Ian indignantly.

'Fancy not taking his wife out since 1972,' said Gillian.

'Yes,' said Ian. 'You would have thought he would have taken her to see ''Watership Down''.'

'The mood she's in, she would probably tell him what he could do with his Watership Down,' I said.

With that we all laughed.

'Are you pleased with the rabbits?' I asked them.

'Yes Sir, they are superb,' said Gillian.

'Lovely,' said Ian.

It was now time for a fairly fast drive back to school before registration. We arrived back with ten minutes to spare, thus saving a lot of explaining to Mr Beech.

Gillian and Ian excitedly took the rabbits out of the boxes and placed them in their new hutches. At morning break the hutches were surrounded by boys and girls of all shapes and sizes and the usual 'Ah look, aren't they sweet?' and 'Look at this little nose

twitching' filled the air. Everyone was delighted with the new arrivals and I was sure when the rabbits had settled in they would be a big hit with the pupils and, like all our animals, get spoiled.

Crystal Grows Up

WE KEPT Crystal on substitute calf milk far too long. We weaned her on the 21st May – she was seven months old. Our Hereford × Friesians are weaned at five or six weeks. I wanted to give Crystal a good start in life – but perhaps I overdid it. Beef calves that will be shown as finished beef animals are often kept on milk or left to suckle a cow until they are many months old, and they look well on it.

Crystal looked well and, to be honest, almost like

a beef calf. As well as milk she was also eating plenty of concentrates, coarse ration – a mixture of protein pellets, flaked maize, linseed cake, oats, barley and mollases – plus the best-quality hay. I had gone too far, she was much too fat for her age. We weaned her – much to her disgust. She made a lot of noise about it, kicking up a terrific din and grumbling in her own way because she thought we had forgotten her. A fortnight later I started to feed her less concentrates. I needed to get the fat off her gradually but at the same time we had to take into consideration that she was still growing, so dieting had to be done slowly.

At the beginning of July she looked like she was supposed to look. I had talked to some Jersey exhibitors at the Three Counties Show and they had told me off for treating her too well. I learned that fat Jerseys do not win prizes.

Crystal now looked good. She had a fine, feminine head and dished face; her shoulders were flat and sloping, with a straight top line from her withers to her tail head; there was excellent body capacity, with hips and pin bones wide apart and good length from her hips to her pin bones. Her four teats were evenly placed and I hoped that one day she would have an udder which would be well developed and run well towards her body. The only fault that I could see was that she stood with her toes facing outwards.

We had all started to halter train her when she was six weeks old, and she became used to going out on the halter at least once a week. Pupils and staff got accustomed to seeing her being taken on these walks around the school grounds as if it were the most natural thing in the world for a Jersey cow to go 'walkies'.

95

I automatically receive show schedules. If you exhibit at a show the secretary will send you the show schedule the following year. For the first time I was looking at cattle classes in addition to the sheep classes.

What I had not realised was that Crystal was really born at the wrong time of the year. Most of the schedules said 'Heifer Calf, to be born on or after 1st January 1988.' This obviously meant Crystal was too old. It was very disappointing. However, we did receive two show schedules which were worded differently. Shustoke Show, near Birmingham, had a class for any breed of heifer calf excluding Friesians (they had their own class) under twelve months old.

Fillongley Show near Coventry had a class for a Jersey heifer calf under twelve months old. I had previously shown sheep at these two shows. We knew them well and we still intended to show sheep at them, but this year we would also show the Jersey calf.

Crystal looked good, but she needed clipping before the shows – quite an easy operation compared with carding and trimming the sheep. The sheep are shampooed once a week before the show season starts. They are worked on each week throughout the show season and the night before the show or on the morning of the show. Crystal would be shown on 30th July and 14th August. I wanted to clip her two weeks before the first show at Shustoke and have her shampooed the day before each show. That would be it – except for a weekly brush. She did not mind this, but her favourite was to have her chin scratched.

Using a borrowed pair of cattle-clipping shears we clipped her ready for the Shustoke Show. We followed tradition and did not clip her all over. We started with the top of her head, then her top line. Next we did her shoulders then her hocks and back legs. Her head, face and ears were last. She looked lovely.

Then on the eve of the show it was bath time. We tied Crystal up and then Carol wet her all over with the hose pipe. She then lathered Crystal with cattle shampoo, being careful not to get any in her eyes. Stuart and Diane rinsed it off and Carol lathered her again; a final rinse and the job was done. I left this job to my pupils as I was busy carding and trimming the sheep. Carol washed her own hair every day so I was confident she would do a good job on Crystal. The recipient of all this attention was not very keen on being washed, probably because she was tied up and could not romp around. But it was a lovely warm evening and she soon dried.

On the morning of the Shustoke Show Carol and Stuart were waiting at the school gates for me. I unlocked them and drove across the playground to the school farm.

The first job was to hitch up the trailer. 'It doesn't look as if Diane is coming,' remarked Carol.

'Yes, it's very strange. It's not like Diane to let us down on the morning of the show,' I agreed. I had only just said it when, on cue, Diane arrived red-faced and breathless.

'You're five minutes late,' said Carol, trying to make her feel guilty.

'You're lucky I'm here at all,' retorted Diane.

'Why, what's wrong?' asked Stuart.

'My alarm clock went off but I went back to sleep again. My mother had to wake me up and I was too late to make any sandwiches.'

'I expect we can help you out,' I said soothingly and feeling very relieved that she had made it in time.

'I've got some mouldy cheese you can have,' offered Stuart.

'Oh thank you very much but no thanks. I'd rather do without,' said Diane, wrinkling her nose in distaste.

After hitching up the trailer we fed the livestock and changed their water. This was done as quickly as possible, and soon it was time to load up. We had previously made a partition for the trailer. Crystal was led in first. She stood on the left-hand side, partitioned off from the sheep that stood on the right side and at the back. Crystal looked beautiful. I half-expected to find that she had lain in her own dung and I imagined having to wash dirty marks and spots off her coat. But no, she was immaculate and did not need any special attention.

Our sheep looked tremendous. We had entered two rams in the same class, Randy Dandy and Jack. We had also entered two ewes, but not as a pair. Shustoke is one of the few shows where ewes are shown individually and so our Bella and Beth were shown as individual entries. The sheep are in mixed classes except for Suffolks, which have classes of their own.

So off we set – showing in a cattle class at a local agricultural show. We had shown sheep many times before but this was a new venture for us. Could we make a success of it? We were hopeful. After all, we had one of nature's beauties riding in our trailer, however, we knew little or nothing about showing cattle.

It was not a long journey and we were soon at the showground. We were early and did not have to queue to get in – in fact we were the first to arrive with sheep. But, as Stuart was keen to point out, some cattle were already there. We could not see any Jerseys.

Unfortunately the cattle were situated away from the sheep. It had already been agreed that Carol would show Crystal. She was the senior pupil and hopefully when Carol left school Diane and Stuart would have a chance to show Crystal or her calf.

'What are we going to do first?' asked Stuart. 'There's so much to get through.'

'Let's get the plastic sheets tied on the inside of the sheep pens,' I said. These were needed to prevent the clean sheep rubbing up against dirty, dusty or rusty rails – we used to use hessian sacks for the same purpose. We tied the sheets up very quickly, put some clean straw in the pen and unloaded the sheep. Randy Dandy was in the first pen, Jack next to him and our two ewes together in the last pen. Randy Dandy had been put in a corner pen with nothing on his left and Jack on his right. True to his name, he could never be trusted. He had only one thought in his head, so I had to try to keep him away from the ewes wherever possible.

Last to leave the trailer was Crystal. Carol proudly led her across the showground to the cattle pens where she had to be tied up in a place allocated to her.

Carol gave her some hay, a bucket of water and some clean straw bedding, and she seemed quite happy. At the same time, Diane, Stuart and myself worked on the four sheep. The sheep judging was to start at ten o'clock, and cattle judging was due to start at the same time; however, Crystal's class was near the end, so with a bit of luck we would have finished showing the sheep before Carol took Crystal into the ring for judging. We were then joined by Phillippa, one of my former pupils. She could now drive and had made her own way to the show to support us. It had been her ambition to be a vet. She had worked hard, and helped out at our local vet's surgery but unfortunately she had not achieved high enough 'A' level grades. She was now working in the laboratories of one of our local hospitals. It was good to see her again. I like my former pupils to keep in touch.

To our chagrin the sheep judging started twenty minutes late. There were twelve entries in the ram class. I thought the judges would never make their decision. Randy Dandy was placed second; Jack was not placed at all. As Diane and I were showing the ewes we could both see Carol in the ring with Crystal, but we were too far away to see properly – and we had to concentrate on what we were doing. Our ewe, Bella, was just 'in the frame', coming fourth. Beth was not placed. Diane was craning her neck to see what was going on in the cattle ring. We were 'on pins' and itching to get over there.

After the rosettes were given out, including a fourth prize for Bella, the steward signalled to us to leave the ring. We made a dignified exit but once outside the ring we tore across to the sheep pens with Bella and Beth in tow. They must have thought this was the ovine equivalent to the Gold Cup or the Greyhound Derby. We had no time to pin up the rosette. We just penned the sheep and made a mad dash to the cattle ring.

Carol was leading Crystal around the ring. To do this, the handler walks backwards and the calf follows. Crystal was behaving perfectly.

'Phew, I thought it would be all over,' panted Diane.

'We haven't missed too much,' I gasped in reply.

The judge called Carol to stand in the centre of the ring. She was the first one to be called out and she stood at the top of the line. I felt an elbow dig in my ribs. Diane was getting excited. The others were then called to stand next to her. The judge handled each calf in turn and stood back to take a long view. The one that stood fourth in line was moved up to third place.

This was nail-biting stuff. At this rate I would soon be down to my wrists. A few of our farming neighbours were watching as well as some of the parents and pupils. It was our first show with Crystal and my heart was hammering. Stuart had his fists clenched. I do not mind admitting – we sweated. Could we win our first show?

The judge then talked to the steward. The steward walked with the rosettes to the top of the line. I held my breath, and Carol was given a rosette. It was the red one. First prize. Crystal had won.

Diane jumped up and down, and screamed with delight, while I fought back the urge to join her. I let go my breath and joined in the round of applause from an appreciative and highly critical audience. Carol, bursting with pride, led Crystal out of the show ring at a stately pace, followed closely by the other exhibitors.

101

Once she was out of the ring pandemonium ruled. Carol was swamped with well-wishers, and cries of 'Well done' and 'Congratulations' filled the air. I am not sure who got the most praise, Carol or the 'star' of the show. I do know that both were thoroughly lapping it up. Phillippa was also very pleased. She congratulated us all.

Because Crystal had won it meant she could go into the calf championship class. Three calves were eligible: the winning Friesian heifer calf, any breed of dairy calf excluding Friesians and the First prize beef calf of any breed.

The three calves were led back into the ring. Both the Friesian and the beef calf, which happened to be a Simmental, belonged to our farming neighbour, Ivan Shorthouse. His was a family farm run by Ivan, his wife, Kathleen, and his mother and father.

Ivan led the beef calf into the ring. It was a bull calf about ten months old and was by far the biggest calf in the class. Next to him stood Kathleen with the Friesian heifer – this one did not in my opinion look like a winner. Our Crystal was last to be led in to the ring. She looked full of herself. The earlier win had really boosted her ego and she looked every inch a champion. The three calves stood in the centre of the ring and then the exhibitors were asked to lead them round. I thought the judge would go for the strong beef calf or the calf with the real dairy quality – our Crystal.

Crystal strutted around – showing herself off. She knew she looked good, and comments from outside the ring were in her favour. The judge signalled to Carol to stand in the centre of the ring. Ivan was asked to stand the Simmental next to her, and third in line was Kathleen with the Friesian heifer. The judge examined each animal again. The atmosphere for me was electric, and all the more exciting because the championship was between our neighbours and ourselves.

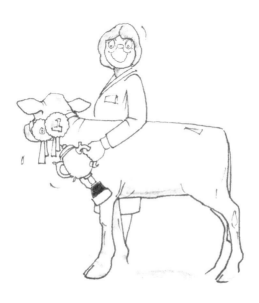

The judge signalled to the steward and it was all over – we had won. The steward gave Carol the red, white and blue Champion Rosette and a cup for the Champion calf in the show. Carol led Crystal back out of the ring triumphantly, two rosettes now pinned to her halter. Carol tied Crystal to the rails. She was surrounded by spectators, pupils, Phillippa, parents

103

and farmers all eager to congratulate her and get a good look at the winner. Diane and I had to fight our way through to get to Carol and Crystal. 'We did it Sir,' she shouted, her face aglow and eyes bright with victory.

'Didn't she do well, Sir?' said Stuart. We were all over the moon. Our sheep had not made such an impact this year, but we had more than made up for it with Crystal.

Ivan had been showing cattle for a number of years at local shows but I had never seen him win a championship with them. His father, Sid, congratulated my pupils and me but Ivan did not. 'Funny, that,' remarked Carol. On close examination of the cup we noticed that in the previous year it had been won by Lord Clifton. We were in exalted company. Minutes later his refined Eton accent rang loud and clear as he congratulated us and made us all promise to keep 'his' cup clean. We were then visited by the press. I took some photographs for our scrap book, and at three o'clock Crystal was taken in the Grand Parade of livestock along with shire horses, Shetland ponies, Hereford cattle and all the other usual breeds. What a wonderful spectacle it was.

Our next show was on 14th August at Fillongley near Coventry. Crystal was entered in the Jersey calf class. There was no championship prize for the champion calf of any breed – but there was a cup to be won for the best Jersey calf; the winner of the Jersey class would automatically get it.

'I wonder if we will win the cup,' pondered Stuart.

'I'm going to do my best,' exclaimed Carol. 'We did it last time.'

Stuart was quick to react. 'Pride comes before a fall.'

'Goeth,' I corrected. 'Pride goeth before a fall.'

I hoped – but I thought it would be too much to ask. We had entered the same four sheep as at Shustoke Show, but this time Bella and Beth would be shown as a pair. As a pair they looked terrific. They had been the Reserve Female Champions at the Royal Show, Montgomeryshire and Three Counties, and first-prize winners at Ashby de la Zouche in Leicestershire – so they stood an excellent chance of winning.

The same format was adopted as before. The pupils washed Crystal on the evening before the show. I met the same three pupils on the morning of the show. They were all at the school gates waiting for me, Diane having been the first to arrive this time.

Traditionally it rains at Fillongley. The sheep pens and cattle lines are not under cover, and we had been soaked on numerous occasions at that show. We wondered if we could hope for a fine day this year. It had made a warm, sunny start, at least.

We unloaded the sheep, then Carol took Crystal off to the cattle lines. They were much further away than at Shustoke, so we would cover a few miles between sheep and cattle in the course of the day.

The sheep were shown in mixed breed classes, except for the Suffolks. Our ram Jack was second. Randy Dandy, much to his disgust, was third in the same class. Our pair of ewes walked away with their class and went on to be the Reserve Champion exhibits in the show, which meant the second-best sheep in the show.

After judging, Stuart, Diane and I left the sheep and went to seek out Carol. She had not yet been in the ring with Crystal.

'Did the sheep win?' she asked.

'Yes. First with the ewes, but we were beaten in the Championship by a Suffolk ram.'

'It's all up to you now to get a Championship with Crystal,' added Stuart.

'I'll do my best. It will look good if the calf does better than the sheep again.'

Carol had brushed Crystal and she looked splendid.

'I felt a spot of rain then,' I said.

They all turned on me. 'Aw, don't say that, Sir. You know about Fillongley's reputation,' they chorused reproachfully.

There were a few more spots of rain, then the heavens opened. The crowd ran every way putting on raincoats, coats, hats and scarves. Umbrellas mushroomed in abundance. The rain lashed viciously across the showground. Tents and marquees bulged to bursting point as the crowds pushed to get out of the wet weather. Up till then the Women's Institute Tent had had very few visitors; now it was bursting at the seams. Stuart and Diane raced back to put plastic sheets on the sheep. Carol tended to Crystal in the same way but the rain was so heavy we could not possibly stand with her. We ran for the nearest tent – no good – it was the beer tent and you could not get in there with a tin opener.

We managed to find room inside the produce tent and looked out at a showground empty except for the bulging tents. Stall holders had tried to cover up their wares with plastic sheeting and had disappeared into their cars and caravans. Fillongley show was living up to its reputation with a vengeance and it looked like being a wash-out yet again. Judging had stopped, and I wondered how long for. I did not want to miss the class. I was wet through now, but I would rather get a complete soaking than miss the judging altogether.

There was no break in the clouds and the loud-speaker crackled to a halt with water in the electrics. Stuart ran back to see if judging had commenced – it had not, and Stuart was wet again. The rain dripped off his coat, soaking his trousers.

By this time I had visions of being towed off the ground. My car and trailer would be about axle deep in mud. Another ten dismal minutes passed by, seeming like two hours. I gazed out over the miserable scene – at least the beer tent was still doing a roaring trade.

'There's a break in the cloud,' said Fillongley's resident Dan Archer optimistically.

'You're right,' I said. The rain eased off – a few brave souls ventured out – most of them straight back to their cars and away home to dry out I assumed. We went back to Crystal; she was fine. Diane and Stuart went back to the sheep. It really did please me to see that my pupils cared about their charges.

The rain stopped but the ground was a mess. Heavy, black clouds hung menacingly overhead with the promise of more rain to come. The friendly sun that had shone so brilliantly for us when we started out had disappeared completely. 'Too bright, too early,' I heard someone say.

It was a good half-hour before the steward asked us to lead Crystal into the ring. Carol put on her white coat which she had managed to keep dry in a plastic bag.

Crystal had got a wet head but most of her back was dry thanks to the plastic sheeting. Carol walked her round the ring – she was certainly very showy. I noticed her feet again. She did tend to walk with her toes facing outwards. Perhaps the judge would not notice, the grass being fairly long. Crystal was doing the school proud – but could we win again?

The judge asked Carol to stand in the centre of the ring – a hopeful sign. The other Jerseys all lined up next to her. A pretty little girl with pigtails stood with a good Jersey in third place. She was only about five years old and was certainly catching the Judge's eye.

'I hope that little girl with the pigtails doesn't get it,' said Stuart seriously.

'Why is that?' asked a farmer who was listening to him.

'Well, in the first place she is not old enough to understand – the calf is sure to belong to her father and I bet that girl is just leading it for today. In the second place, I bet she does not feed it twice a day and muck out its shed or groom it for shows.' He was really into his stride.

'Well, she's a good girl for five or six years old,' said the farmer. 'She handles that calf well for her age.'

'The class isn't being judged on handling; it's being judged on points of the calf,' said Diane, obviously on Stuart's side.

A horrible thought crossed my mind: was this man the child's father? I did not want to get involved in

108

any arguments, I just wanted Crystal to win. So I kept out of it and left them to get on with it. The judge handled each calf in turn and then quickly signalled to the steward to give out the rosettes. They both walked over to Carol and Crystal standing at the top of the line – out of the plastic bag came the red rosette. We had won. The judge and steward continued down the line giving out rosettes to fourth place. They then returned to the table in the centre of the ring – picked up the cup and presented it to Carol along with the red, white and blue rosette. Crystal was the Champion Jersey calf in the show. Carol again proudly led her back with two more rosettes tied to her halter. We were again visited by the press. I took some more photographs. I had only taken a couple when large spots of rain hit the camera lens. It was going to rain heavily again. It had kept fine for the judging but we were going to get another downpour. Fortunately it cleared up for the Grand Parade and again Crystal went into the ring with all the other champions.

Many exhibitors had now gone home. After the parade we decided to do the same; we had all had enough. We loaded Crystal into the trailer and we were just getting her comfortable when the judge appeared and joined us in the trailer.

'That's a fine Jersey calf you have there, Miss,' he said to Carol.

'Yes, she certainly is,' said Carol, looking pleased.

'I can't fault her. You must have a huge herd to breed one as good as that,' he said.

'Well actually, we haven't,' said Diane.

'Haven't what?' he asked, looking a little bewildered.

109

'Got a herd,' said Diane.

'How many cows have you got then?' he queried.

'We haven't any cows,' said Stuart. 'Just this one calf.'

'Ah, I see. You bought her. Well she's a fine animal. Can I have the name and address of the breeder you bought her from? I could do with some like her in my own herd.'

'Actually we bought her from Her Majesty the Queen,' said Carol.

'Her address is Buckingham Palace,' I added, determined not to be left out of the conversation.

'You're having me on,' he said.

'No we're not. It's Buckingham Palace,' I continued.

'No, really. Crystal did come from the royal herd at Windsor, but it's a one-off. The Queen doesn't normally sell calves to school farms.'

'I don't think I'll bother trying,' he sighed, and with that disappeared into the remaining crowd.

It was a great end to the show. Crystal had been excellent. Two shows, two first prizes, two championships and two cups. She was unbeaten.

The following Monday I telephoned the manager at the Royal Farms. He was delighted with our success and I promised to send him some photographs of the shows. I hoped he would pass them on to Crystal's original owner.

Crystal grew well in the autumn and winter, and she continued to be a favourite with the pupils. I now had more pupils interested in her and they shared the workload.

Half of her building was bedded with straw for her to lie on; the other half was scraped out with a shovel and then brushed twice a day.

After Christmas I had to make some decisions as to her future. What would we do with her milk? I telephoned the Milk Marketing Board and they gave me the telephone number of the local adviser, a Mr Terry Prewett. He came and looked at Crystal and the building she was in. He explained that there would be a lot of red tape if I wanted to produce butter and cheese for human consumption, and he recommended that I contact the Ministry of Agriculture, so that they could give me the real facts. He wished me luck but suggested I feed all the milk to the pigs or calves.

I wrote to the Ministry of Agriculture at Leamington Spa. In due course I received a letter from the Dairy Husbandry Advisor, explaining that in order to produce milk other than for domestic consumption by a private individual, the school must be registered with the Ministry of Agriculture, Fisheries and Food. Our premises and methods of milk production must comply with the Milk and Dairies (General) Regulations 1959. The Dairy Husbandry Adviser would pay us an initial visit to see if our premises could be registered. After the first call, routine visits would be made at intervals of one to three years or every nine months for untreated licence holders – at a cost of eighty pounds per visit. We were advised that there could be health risks from untreated milk and milk products – it was recently announced that the sale of untreated milk would probably be banned. In other words, the milk would have to be pasteurised. Pasteuring equipment could cost as much as ten thousand pounds. The

Ministry also stated that I would have to be registered with the Milk Marketing Board; Terry Prewett had, of course, told me this. Before I could sell butter and cheese we would need to purchase a direct sales quota. (A quota is in existence to stop farmers producing lakes of milk and mountains of butter and cheese.) To buy a quota to produce four thousand litres of milk a year would cost about two hundred pounds.

Regulations and the costs were stacked against us and the necessity to pay eighty pounds a visit for the Dairy Husbandry Adviser was outrageous. I wished that I could charge eighty pounds for a consultation at parents' evening! At forty sets of parents a time! In view of all the outlay I decided not to bother with the sale of dairy produce. We could always make some butter and cheese as a class project and then feed it to the pigs. However, it was obvious the liquid milk had to be fed to pigs and calves.

I telephoned Terry Prewett and told him of my decision. He thought I had made the wisest choice. However, I did want the Milk Marketing Board to officially record Crystal's milk yields. This involves a milk recorder coming on to the farm once a month to record yields. We wanted this doing officially so that we could have some records to go on Crystal's pedigree.

Soon after making this decision, one of my farming friends, Richard Jonas, informed me of a portable milking machine for sale at a smallholding in Tamworth Staffordshire.

I telephoned Mr Sturmey, who told me I could view the machine but that the price was four hundred pounds and I was not to insult him by offering less.

I hitched the trailer on to the car the next evening and went to view the machine. It was, as the owner said, 'like new'. It consisted of a galvanised milking bucket with teat cups and an electric motor. The machine was simply plugged in and switched on. It had been used for a few months only to milk a single Jersey, but as Mr Sturmey suffered from asthma – and it was thought that the cow had made him ill – the Jersey was sold. That was two years ago. The milking machine had certainly been looked after and it was in immaculate condition. We actually viewed it where it was stored in a spare bedroom. We plugged it in and it worked perfectly.

At the great risk of offending Mr Sturmey I offered him three hundred and fifty pounds for it. It was a bit cheeky because the original price included a home-made trolley for easy movement. Mr Sturmey said 'No,' he wanted the four hundred pounds. This was a lot of money for us to find but I realised a brand-new machine would probably cost twice that amount.

I said I was sorry we could not do business and started to walk down the stairs.

'All right,' he called, 'I'll take the three hundred and fifty pounds. I suppose I haven't got the job of advertising it.' I paid him and loaded it up – with the trolley – and put it in store. After all, we would not be needing it for about another twelve or thirteen months.

In late February I telephoned the Royal Farms and spoke to the herdsman. Crystal was now sixteen months old and would soon be ready to breed with. As promised, I did not take her to the bull that 'lives just down the road'. Trevor Burwood, the herdsman, suggested we use one of the Queen's superior bulls, Ferdons Glen Lionheart. He agreed to send out the semen. Semen is kept in straws and stored at their local Artificial Insemination Centre run by the Milk Marketing Board.

Trevor told me I needed to get on to our local AI centre to register with them and then three straws would be transferred from one AI centre to the other. The three straws would cost us £25.88 including VAT. A form was sent to the school which I completed. Needless to say it was returned post haste. The semen was then transferred and was there ready and waiting.

When Crystal came on heat, or was bulling as it is called, I needed to telephone our local AI centre and the semen would be inseminated into her on that day by an experienced operator. An adult cow is on heat for about twenty-four hours. Maiden heifers are

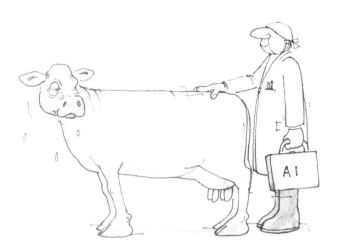

seldom on heat for more than twelve hours. If cows are in a group, a cow on heat can be detected by her standing to be ridden by another cow. Obviously with only one heifer this is not possible, so we looked for other signs, the main one being frequent bawling. We made a note on the farm calendar of the day she bawled a lot and sure enough twenty days later she bawled again. The heifer or cow will come on heat every twenty days until she is in calf. We were now all organised and ready for the AI man.

Dabbling With the Ducks

MY PUPILS were very disappointed.

'Sir – Sir – the incubator has broken down and all the eggs have gone cold,' said the very upset boy I met just before assembly one morning.

On examination it was certainly not working – it was still plugged in but there was no sign of life. Worn out I imagined; it was rather aged. I listened to some expert advice from an ex-pupil turned electrician and he told me it was ready for the scrap heap. With this old incubator we had to turn the eggs three times a day. Each egg was marked with a cross on one side and a circle on the other; this made it easy to see which eggs had been turned. In their natural state the eggs would be turned automatically by the parent birds. My pupils would turn them before school started, again when school finished and I would turn them a third time just before bedtime. This last turning at night was quite an inconvenience but I did not really mind as I always check the livestock at bedtime anyway. However, turning about three dozen eggs one by one seems a very time-consuming occupation. I do not think I ever forgot, but I know some of the pupils forgot occasionally.

So, it was time to invest in a new incubator. I wanted a good one. One that would last and one that would turn the eggs for us. There are some cheap plastic ones on the market but, after comparing one with the other, I finally decided on a fine looking piece of equipment of mahogany construction with a perspex top, electric controls and a heating element. It was large enough to hold sixty eggs. It set us back one hundred and forty pounds but it was well worth every penny. We placed it on a bench in the classroom for all to see and plugged it in.

'Can we put the eggs in, Sir?' asked Robert.

'No, not yet. We will run it empty at first to make sure it's working properly and the temperature is right,' I said.

It was a good job we did because the temperature went right off the scale and would have cooked the eggs. To adjust it we had to move a dial at the back of the incubator. We adjusted it but it was still too high so it had to be turned down again. After this second adjustment the heat dropped to a steady 38 degrees Celsius but we still left it empty for forty-eight hours, just to be on the safe side. I put a couple of infertile hen eggs in to make sure the turning mechanism was working. It was, so we were ready to introduce the eggs.

I find that pupils have little or no knowledge of birds' eggs or incubation. Many birds start to sit on their eggs after the last one has been laid. You can find a mallard's nest in the wild with four eggs in it and they will be cold. I have heard of boys collecting eggs from the nests and saying, 'It doesn't matter because there were only a few eggs and they were cold.' It does matter, though, because this does not mean the mother bird has deserted her

117

nest; she will lay some more eggs. In the case of the mallard she will lay probably another three eggs and then she will start to incubate. Of course, if they go cold after incubation has started then the embryos will die.

Eggs are usually laid early in the morning. Small species lay them at twenty-four hour intervals, larger species lay their eggs at two-day intervals, and some really large species at four-day intervals. Many birds start to 'sit' after the clutch has been laid – all the young then hatch together and are similar in size so each has a fair chance of competing against its brothers and sisters for food. Other species, including owls, start to incubate after the first egg has been laid; therefore, the first bird to hatch will be a lot bigger and stronger than the last one. If it is a season when prey is scarce then the younger birds will die while the older ones – or one – will get bigger and stronger.

My pupils collected the duck eggs and hen eggs. We store them in a cupboard for a week or more and then put them in the incubator. At first my pupils think they have gone cold and will not hatch – they soon learn the facts though.

'How long do eggs take to hatch, Sir?' asked Robert.

'It varies with the species,' I replied.

'Do they hatch quicker in an incubator than under the mother?' asked Amanda.

'No, it's the same, and before you ask – No, they won't hatch quicker if you put them in a microwave oven,' I said. I would not put it past them to try.

Incubation periods differ greatly. A robin incubates

for about two weeks while a swan incubates for about five weeks. A newly hatched robin is blind, naked and 'nidicolous', which means that it will be looked after in the nest. Some birds (termed 'nidifugous') leave the nest soon after hatching, baby ducks among them. They hatch with their eyes open, are covered with down and can walk and swim. The mother duck does not desert them, though; the ducklings will follow her and they will rest and sleep under her wings. She will shelter them from rain and sun, defend them against predators and guide them to food. They soon learn what to eat.

Our two female Aylesbury ducks made nests in their pen during early March, and started to lay. They were careful to cover and hide their eggs when they went outside. Jeremy, our Aylesbury drake, could be seen from the classroom mating with our ducks. He would sometimes mate with them on the side of the pond but usually in the water. Here he would climb on their backs and hold the back of their necks in his beak sometimes forcing the duck's head under water. 'He's drowning her, Sir,' my pupils would cry out in alarm. A young lady teacher of mathematics borrowed my classroom for one lesson when I had a free period. Her pupils lost concentration completely and she was so embarrassed by the antics going on in the duck pond her face was red for nearly a fortnight. Jeremy certainly knew how to multiply. We expected fertile eggs.

After we had introduced the eggs into the incubator the temperature dropped slightly but we did not alter the controls because the eggs needed to get warmed up. For the first twenty-four hours the eggs

119

are not turned, then the turning switch stays on – the incubator then turns the eggs automatically. After the fifth day of incubating we made the atmosphere more humid by half-filling the water trays which stand in the incubator.

A few years ago one of our parents made us an egg candler. This consists of a black wooden box with a small round hole at the front rather like a blue tit's nesting box. Inside is a light bulb. When the candler is turned on the light shines out of the hole very brightly and intensively.

To use the candler efficiently we wait until it is dark, plug in the candler and hold the eggs up to the hole. The light is so bright we can see through the shell and, if the egg is fertile, we can see the embryo growing inside. We candled all our thirty eggs at five days and again a couple of days later. Seven of them were infertile and these were thrown out. We candled them again on the 14th and 18th days to remove any dead embryos, of which there were none – all the eggs looked healthy.

One of my second-year classes was in charge of the incubator – checking the temperature twice a day and making sure the water trays contained water. They looked forward to the time when the eggs were due to hatch. The incubation period for a duck egg is twenty-eight days. Three days before hatching, the turning rods in the incubator were removed and the eggs placed in the special hatching trays. The switch operating the turning rods was switched off. 'Will we have to help them out of their shells?' asked one pupil.

'The ducklings should have no trouble hatching

without any assistance. I have helped them in the past but if you are not careful you make them bleed. If the ducklings are well developed and fit they will manage,' I said.

'If you hold the egg up to your ear a day or so before hatching is due you may be able to hear the young duckling calling inside the shell.'

'How do they actually get out of the shell?' asked Paul.

'The young chicks develop a horny implement called an egg tooth on the tip of the beak which enters the air space inside the shell; it is used like a pick to puncture the shell. Once the shell has been opened the duckling presses hard with its head and legs until the shell cracks and breaks even more. All this takes several hours, and after hatching the egg tooth disappears,' I explained. My pupils were fascinated and listened to me with rapt expressions on their faces. It was even more magical for them when they held some of the eggs up to their ears and heard the ducklings calling. The incubation of eggs is a marvellous educational aid and very worthwhile.

When our eggs started to chip we filled both water trays with warm water and closed the incubator air vent down to setting number two to build up humidity. To maintain the valuable humidity, the incubator was then left until most of the eggs had hatched. Young ducklings and chickens can live quite comfortably in the incubator for up to two days without food and water; however, in practice we open the lid and take ours out before they are twenty-four hours old. Nineteen ducklings hatched out of the remaining twenty-three eggs; the other four eggs unfortunately had dead embryos inside – this is known as 'dead in shell'.

We transferred the young ducklings into the new quarters in a pen which is round because otherwise young birds will crowd into corners and suffocate. To keep them warm we gave them an infra-red lamp. We put plenty of straw on the floor and some damp chick crumbs and water in containers to get the ducklings off to a good start. Christopher and Nicholas were our chief 'duck keepers'.

The next day Mrs Loveridge, the school secretary, came over the playground to my classroom. 'Mr Terry – a Mr Smith has telephoned from Coventry. He's got a pair of mallards you can have.'

'Oh, I don't think we want them as I've just had nineteen ducklings hatch out in our incubator,' I replied.

'Well if you don't have them he's just going to kill

them and put them in the freezer.'

'He didn't say how old they were, did he?' I asked.

'Yes, he did as a matter of fact, Mr Terry. They are just twelve months old. He says they will be ready to breed from at any time,' she said, then went on, 'I'm more like a farm secretary every day.'

I thanked her very much and told her that I would telephone Mr Smith at break that morning.

This I did to find the ducks were to be a gift. Not one to look a gift horse in the mouth I accepted his offer very gratefully and said I would collect them the next day, which would be Saturday. He said that he had got a few more ducks to sell if I was interested, but I thought we would have enough.

I told one of my farming friends – Richard Jonas. He was very enthusiastic and said he would like some mallards to go on his farm pond. Richard wanted to come with me and agreed to pick me up in his Land Rover the next morning. I had almost finished feeding the livestock, ably assisted by some of my pupils, when Richard arrived. He had not changed his clothes after milking and smelt very strongly of cattle, much to my pupils' amusement.

Christopher had gone away for the weekend with his parents, so it was left to Nicholas to feed the ducklings, which he was doing when Richard arrived. We went over to look at the ducklings and when I explained to Nicholas what we were going to do he was eager to come with us. We had to wait while he checked with his parents because originally he had been going to go into town with his mother to buy a new pair of trousers. He returned with a smile of triumph on his face – the trousers could wait until the afternoon.

The three of us set off – Richard drove but there was easily enough room in the front for Nicholas and myself. I enjoy riding in a Land Rover, you sit higher than in a car and you can 'farm' other farmers' fields by looking over the hedges.

This vehicle was certainly a farm machine – it reminded me of Bert's car or Mick Hardy's old van, with hay and straw all over the floor and an assortment of spanners, screws, nails and bolts in the glove compartment – although the Land Rover was not in quite such a state as the two former vehicles.

The smallholding belonging to Mr Smith took some finding. I asked a builder who was laying bricks for a house extension for directions to the smallholding. As I spoke to him for a fleeting moment I thought his face looked familiar.

'. . . and so that's the way to go . . . Mr Terry.'

I looked closely at him as he had used my name. 'I thought your face was familiar,' I said. 'I know you now. It's Raymond Huntington, isn't it?'

'That's right, Mr Terry' he replied, and looked pleased that I had remembered him. How could I forget him! Raymond Huntington of all people. When I had first made his acquaintance he was only sixteen but had a record as long as your arm; if it was not nailed down Raymond Huntington would steal it. The trouble was he wore his misdemeanours like a badge of honour and would openly brag about his goings on to anyone who would stop and listen. He was a young lad with all the signs of becoming an old lag. Oh yes, I would certainly remember Raymond Huntington.

'Are you still running the school farm, Mr Terry?' he enquired politely.

'I certainly am,' I replied. 'Do you live around here then?'

'No, I live with my wife and two children nearer to town.'

We had quite a pleasant little chat then. It appeared he was a builder by trade and was doing a job, legitimately, for someone and that was why he hesitated in his directions to the smallholding. He had married a local girl and they had a son and a daughter. It is great to meet up with my old pupils, especially when I realise they have turned out alright.

I said cheerio to Raymond and, following his directions, we soon found Mr Smith's smallholding.

We went down a short drive. The house was superb. Snowcemed and with new windows and doors, plus a large extension, it seemed to welcome all-comers. It was obvious a lot of care and money had been lavished on it. The rear of the house looked out onto the stable yard. It was neat and tidy with a dozen or more stables, but only one pony.

We met Mr Smith and shook hands with him – he was a representative for double glazing and, judging by his own house, he was a good advertisement for his firm.

He took the three of us into a field at the side of the house – here was a duck pond with mallards, Aylesburys and Indian runner ducks, Emden and Canadian geese.

'Have we got to catch these ducks from off the pond?' I asked – dreading the answer.

'No, Mr Terry. I've got your pair of mallards locked in the shed.'

'Splendid,' I said, breathing a sigh of relief.

'Actually – I would like to purchase a pair of mallards for my farm pond – would you have a pair handy or would we have to catch them?' asked Richard.

I hoped we did not have to catch them because the ones I could see were metres away swimming contentedly in the middle of the pond. We all had Wellingtons on but it was very, very muddy. If one of us slipped, he would try to grab hold of someone else, who in turn would try to grab another person, who in turn, etc. We would have a domino effect of one person taking another one down into the water.

'You are in luck,' said Mr Smith. 'I've got another pair in my other shed – a gentleman was going to collect them yesterday but he didn't turn up. I'm giving Mr Terry his but I will only charge you £1.50 each,' he said.

'That's great,' replied Richard.

I looked at the ducks that he had sorted out for the school. 'What do you think to those Nicholas?' I asked.

'They're lovely,' he beamed. 'Especially the drake – he looks really smart.'

He did look smart. He had a bottle-green head with a white collar and brown breast, grey under parts and a white tail with black centre feathers. He would be a real contrast to our Aylesburys.

The duck was mottled brown – but both drake and duck had a purple speculum between two white bars. (The speculum is the name for a patch of feathers on the wing of a duck and these are marked differently in colour from the surrounding feathers.)

'They are lovely – we will take them. Thank you very much,' I said.

'They won't fly off because I've clipped their wings,' he said confidently.

Mr Smith put the ducks in a cardboard box for us. We then looked at the ones he was going to sell Richard – they were superb as well. Mr Smith put them in another box. Richard paid him; we put both boxes in the back of the Land Rover. We thanked him once again and started the return journey back to school.

The two boxes of ducks were quite safe in the open Land Rover. Mr Smith had tied the boxes with string. We had a pleasant journey back. The sun was shining and we were pleased with our new purchases.

We had reached the suburbs of town when Nicholas looked behind him out of the back window of the Land Rover.

'Er, I don't want to alarm you Sir, but we've got a lorry load of mallards in the back there.'

'What!' shouted Richard.

'Let me see,' I said. I looked out of the back and there standing on the metal floor of the open-backed Land Rover were a duck and a drake. I could see the empty box too – they had forced their way out of the top. So much for Mr Smith's packaging! It was the school's ducks, not Richard's, which had escaped.

'I can't stop, there's traffic right up behind me, and I can't pull over,' said Richard.

It was a built-up area and a main road. A huge lorry was behind us with a smiling lorry driver pointing to the two escaped ducks and thoroughly enjoying every minute of the 'cabaret' that had suddenly come to enlighten what was probably to him just another

mundane journey. By this time the drake was feeling confident and was fluffing up his feathers and starting to quack; he was also stretching his neck to see. At last Richard was able to stop the Land Rover and waved the traffic on. As soon as the Land Rover stopped the ducks flew out and landed between cars a few metres up the road. They could not fly properly as their wings had been clipped, but it was enough to cause trouble. A car stopped then moved on again, the car in the opposite direction kept on coming. We would be lucky to get the ducks off the road in one piece.

I had kept cage birds, bantams and ducks when I was a lad and also poultry since teaching at my school, and I prided myself on being able to catch them.

128

However, it looked as if a flying rugby tackle was the order of the day where these two were concerned. The ducks waddled through the traffic, closely followed by the three of us. Then they were sensible enough to find some refuge on the pavement. As soon as we got within a couple of metres of them they would run off again. We would never catch them like that. We needed to corner them. Richard crossed the road.

'I'll run up here, get in front of them, then walk back on your side of the road,' he said. 'We can try and corner them in someone's front garden.' I hoped the 'someone' would be out as I did not think they would be very happy at two ducks and three humans trampling over their prize pansies.

These were small gardens in front of the terraced houses. Richard moved quickly and started to walk towards the ducks. An old couple stood at their garden gate on the other side of the road watching in amusement and a little boy about four years old tugged frantically at his mother's sleeve to look at the ducks. I hoped he did not think he would get the chance to feed them with bread.

The ducks turned to their right into a front garden and waddled up to the front door. I had caught one of them within a short time and Nicholas caught the other, both of us making sure we held our hands on top of their wings to stop them flapping about. We were just in time – a big black labrador dog came bouncing up to us and jumped at Nicholas. The drake was frightened half to death, but Nicholas was holding him tightly.

'Go away dog,' shouted Richard at the top of his voice and the dog turned and ran with its tail between its legs. I could see that Richard was losing his temper.

'Let's get these back into the box,' I said. Richard opened it and Nicholas and myself placed the ducks inside. We tied the box up tightly with string and then checked that the other box was secure.

'I'm taking no chances,' I said. 'Nicholas and I will sit with the boxes on our laps.' We did, and we had no further problems.

The two mallards looked good on our school pond but the Aylesburys soon showed them who ruled the roost. The females fought one another and Jeremy the Aylesbury drake had to mate with the mallard duck to show he was dominant, but they soon settled down.

A week after our ducklings had hatched Nicholas asked me if he could clean them out. 'Yes,' I replied. 'Is Christopher going to help you?'

'I don't think so, Sir. He's losing interest in them.'

I had not seen Christopher feeding the ducklings as often as Nicholas, but this sometimes happens. I cannot always keep all the helpers interested in their own time; they often have other interests which may come first.

School had only just finished for the day, so Christopher could still turn up to help. However, I left Nicholas to work on his own, as he was a capable lad, and busied myself with the sheep. I walked past Nicholas who was taking the ducklings out of their pen and putting them in a small cardboard box where they would be out of the way while he changed the straw. I looked at the size of the box – it was very small.

'Nicholas, you won't get them all in that box – find

somewhere else to put some of them but don't let them get cold,' I said.

'Don't worry, Mr Terry. I'll manage,' he replied.

I fed the sheep and walked back past the ducklings to find them in the cardboard box with an infra-red light over them. It looked as though work had started on cleaning out the pen – but Nicholas had vanished. I thought he had gone to the toilet, and I knew he would finish the job.

Ten minutes later he still had not returned. I asked all the pupils who had stayed behind on the school farm if they had seen Nicholas. 'No Sir,' was the reply every time.

Then Christopher turned up: 'Sorry I'm late, Sir. I went home to get changed.'

'That's alright – Nicholas has started to clean the ducklings out but he's disappeared,' I said.

'That's unlike him,' remarked Christopher.

'Yes it is,' I agreed.

Christopher set to and took out all the soiled bedding. He replaced it with clean straw and put the ducklings back.

I was looking at Crystal when Christopher came running up to me. 'Sir, Sir. There's five ducklings missing,' he gasped.

'Don't be silly. How can there be? Go and count them again.'

'I've counted them three times. I tell you, Sir. There's five missing.'

I followed him to the classroom. We took each duckling out of its pen in turn and put it in a cardboard box – it was the easiest and most methodical way to count them. There were fourteen.

'Sir, where do you think they have gone?'

We counted them back into their pen and still came up with the same answer. Fourteen.

By this time some of the other pupils had heard us and they all started looking for the five missing ducklings. They looked everywhere but there was no sign of them.

'Do you think Nicholas has stolen the ducklings and run off with them?' asked Diane.

'No. He wouldn't do a thing like that,' I replied confidently.

'Well, where can he be?' she asked in vain.

'Oh. I've just thought, Mr Terry. He should be in detention,' said Christopher. Now he tells me!

'I need to find out what he's done with those ducklings,' I said. 'I'll go and find him.'

Detention at our school is traditionally held on Thursday from 3.45 until 4.15. We have a staff rota so a different member of staff is in charge of it each week. I had no idea who was in charge today. Each pupil has to sit at his or her own desk and the member of staff who has put that pupil in detention will have set that pupil some work – which is usually an essay on mending their ways. I had no idea what Nicholas was in detention for and I was not even sure I was going to find him there. I walked across the playground, into the school and along the corridor.

As I approached a classroom I could hear Mr Petty's voice, and as I got nearer I could see through the glass. Nicholas was standing at the front and Mr Petty was really telling him off. I walked into the classroom just in time to hear Mr Petty say, 'Who the devil do you think you are, Boy? Merlin the Magician?' I could see why – there on the teacher's desk, making quite a racket, were my missing ducklings. Well, three of them anyway. Which was a start.

'And what have we got in this pocket?' asked Mr Petty. 'A white rabbit, or perhaps a dove or maybe even a feather duster . . .' he said sarcastically.

Nicholas sheepishly put his hand in his pocket and produced another duckling. He placed it carefully on the desk with the others. He then put his hand back in his pocket and brought out the last duckling.

'Oh my stars,' said Mr Petty, despairingly. 'Is that the lot now?'

'That's the lot now,' replied Nicholas.

'Are you sure?' persisted Mr Petty.

'I'm sure,' he replied.

'That's right,' I interrupted. 'There were five missing.'

Then Mr Petty turned on me: 'Well, Mr Terry. For your information I had twelve boys and girls all sitting in here carrying out their detention and getting on with some written work.' It was fine. You could hear a pin drop. Suddenly, I heard a kind of cheeping, whistling sound. At first I thought it was the birds outside the classroom window but the noise continued – louder – definitely in the classroom. I asked the person responsible to stop making the bird impressions. It didn't stop and no one owned up. I waited and still it continued.

I then told the twelve that if the person responsible didn't come out to the front immediately they would all be in serious trouble. Nicholas came out to the front and said it wasn't him it was the ducks in his pocket. I didn't believe him – I said he was lying. Then he produced one – like a magician – straight out of his pocket, and then another one. I said ''I've got ducks in detention lad – and I'm not having it.'' Then you came in, Mr Terry. So now that you're here perhaps Nicholas can explain more fully.' The other eleven pupils had stopped work and were craning their necks to see the ducklings.

'Get back to work the rest of you. I can see you sniggering and grinning. It's nothing to laugh at,' ranted Petty. The other eleven pupils began to write again.

'Now then, Nicholas, explain yourself – in front of Mr Terry and me.' Before he started, I scooped up the five ducklings and put them in the empty waste paper bin. They had come to no harm.

'I started to clean the ducks out, moving the ducklings out of their pen and placing them in a cardboard box. Mr Terry said the box was too small for all of them and they must not get cold. I put fourteen in the box and moved the infra-red lamp so that it kept them warm. I then put three in my left trouser pocket and two in the right trouser pocket. It was cosy in there for them and my legs would keep them warm. I suddenly realised that I was in detention. I was a few minutes late. I knew it was Mr Petty in charge of detention this week, and you can't be late for him because he's strict. I ran up to do my detention. I knew the others under the lamp would be alright and I didn't think these would make a noise. I was going to finish cleaning them all out after I had done my detention.'

'You have disturbed the others in this detention,' remarked Petty.

'Sorry, Sir,' said Nicholas. 'I didn't mean to.'

'Yes, and I have been worried sick searching high and low for these ducklings,' I said.

'I really am very sorry Sir.'

'You can do an extra detention next Thursday,' declared Petty.

'Yes, another detention next week,' I agreed.

'I will. I promise I will,' he vowed.

'Sit down and finish your work. I'll take the duck-lings back to the school farm – Christopher is finishing off your job there,' I said.

Nicholas sat down and started to write, the others were working hard. I picked up the litter bin contain-ing the ducklings. I thanked Mr Petty but all he could mutter was, 'ducks in detention – I just don't believe it. I can see now why Mr Beech wants to teach at a "normal" school.'

I returned to the school farm, and on my way back all I could think about were Mr Petty's words, 'It's nothing to laugh at'. I suppose he was right really, but as soon as I was out of earshot I threw my head back and had a really good laugh about it. I visualised Nicholas in a tall pointed hat and long flowing black cloak with cabalistic symbols all over it producing ducklings from every pocket in sight.

I returned the ducklings to Christopher; he had finished cleaning them out by the time Nicholas returned from his detention.

'What were you in detention for?' I asked him.

'Talking, Sir. In my maths class,' he replied.

'What were you talking about?' I asked.

'Ducks, Sir. Ducks,' was his reply.

Our nineteen ducklings grew well. We wanted to keep two females, an ex-pupil, Alan Davies, was interested in purchasing a pair, and I was hoping to sell the other fifteen to our local poultry farmer, Derek Crawford. He is the farmer from whom we buy our chickens. He would rear the ducks for 'duck dinners'. I was not interested in rearing them as they are such difficult creatures to pluck. It takes such a long time I find that it is not worth the bother.

When the ducks were about eight weeks old, I delivered a pair to Alan Davies. He was now married with two children. Alan met me at the garden gate of his council house and was eager to show me the pond he had made ready for them in the back garden.

'It's not lined with plastic, is it?' I asked remembering the time I dug out a pond with the aid of my pupils. I lined it with plastic sheeting and the ducks almost shredded it with the claws on their webbed feet.

'No, it's a concrete pond,' replied Alan.

'Oh yes?' I said doubtfully and raised my eyebrows, but thereby hangs another tale.

We started towards the duck pond when Alan's wife Helen came out to meet us. She had an Alsatian with her called Jill.

'That's a lovely looking dog,' I remarked.

'She's beautiful, isn't she. She's new. Her previous owner couldn't do anything with her. She's got an excellent pedigree but they were going to have her destroyed. She's had a reprieve now.'

The dog jumped up me and almost knocked the box of ducks out of my hands.

'Get down and behave yourself,' I commanded the

dog. With that Helen called the dog and shut her in the kitchen.

We then walked over to the pond. It was small compared with ours, but it would be quite adequate for two ducks. Alan had built them a fine pen to house them for the night. We let them out of their box – and then Helen rejoined us.

The two ducks walked nervously around their new enclosure. One had a drink out of the pond, but they did not venture into it.

'I want to see them have a swim,' lisped Helen imitating a little girl's voice. After five or so minutes she could wait no longer and drove them towards the water. They plunged in, quacking loudly and flapped their wings. 'They will be all right,' said Alan.

I left them the empty cardboard box to get rid of, collected the money and drove back to school. I would deliver the others to Derek Crawford the next evening.

The next day I went home for my tea before delivering Derek Crawford's ducks. I had just finished my meal when the telephone rang.

'Hello John, it's Helen. I've got some bad news for you.' Echoes of Lord Clifton's call about the lambs came drifting home.

'We got home at five this afternoon and found Jill roaming around the garden with a head and feathers of a duck in her mouth. We obviously checked the ducks and I'm sorry to say she has killed them both. Alan has taken her to the vet to have her put down. I know it's a shame but let's face it, John, the next victim could have been one of the children. I daren't risk it.'

137

'I'm sorry to hear this, Helen,' I said. This was a re-enactment of the episode of Lord Clifton and his dog, Charlie.

'Well the dog has gone now. So can I buy two more ducks, please?' she asked.

'I've agreed to sell the rest to Derek Crawford, but I'll give him a call and see if we can arrange something,' I promised.

Derek Crawford was most obliging and agreed to let two of the fifteen ducks go to Alan and Helen.

The new ducks settled in well in their new home and they have had no further problems.

We are now looking forward to hatching out some more eggs in our incubator. I hope we do not get as many problems next time. And I shall try to see that none of the new ducklings get detention.

Vicky

IT WAS the 27th March and it was pouring with rain. My pupils and I fed the livestock quickly so that we could get indoors. I sat in my classroom marking my register, my hair was wet through, water trickling down my back, my socks squelched in my shoes and my trousers stuck to my legs. Not a very auspicious start to the day.

Lambing had nearly finished and in fact we had not had any lambs born for a couple of days; although Sarah the goat had kidded the day before. She had produced two lovely little nannies. I was almost half-way through my register when John Green knocked on my door, came in and stood beside me at my desk. He was carefully clutching a shoe box, the lid held in place by string. John would have to wait for a few minutes until I had completed my register and sent my pupils to assembly. But I noticed that this box had holes punched in the lid, so I knew it contained something live; I could not help losing concentration and wondering what was in the box.

John would know better than to bring me a young fledgling. Children do pick up fledglings. They see a bird which cannot fly very well but just seems to flap around on the floor, so they pick it up and take it home, thinking it is injured or abandoned. In fact it has just flown from the nest, is still being fed by the mother and is perfectly all right. The young bird should be left alone. My pupils are given lessons on this soon after they attend our school. Perhaps John had got an injured bird, an adult; perhaps a sparrow, blackbird or starling.

John was a small boy but seemed as hard as nails. He had dark, greasy hair, a round face with red cheeks. He had a love of the countryside. He did not come to the school farm in his own time very often. He liked the farm but he did not have much time; after school he was keen to get home and take the dogs out. His family had three: a lurcher bitch, a black labrador dog and a Jack Russell terrier bitch. John's father enjoyed shooting and John would accompany him on pheasant shoots during the winter weekends. John had asked me on a couple of occasions if I would rear a few pheasants, or dig out a large pool, stock it with fish and let him have the fishing rights. He also kept ferrets and said he would bring one of these in to show the class. I hoped it was not a ferret in the box. An angry ferret can almost take your finger off. I did not think it was a ferret – so what could it be?

I finished marking my register, sent my pupils off to assembly and turned to face John.

'What can I do for you then, John?' I asked.

'I've brought an orphan in for you,' he said, handing me the box at the same time.

'An orphan what?' I asked.

'Wait and see Sir, you won't half be surprised. Go on, have a look.'

I rested the box on the table, moved the lid cautiously and peeped inside.

'You can take the lid off, Sir. It won't jump out at you,' said John.

I took the lid off, and there, lying inside almost motionless, was a baby fox cub. It lay on its side and it was obviously unwell. It did not look like a fox cub and to the inexperienced eye it could have been mistaken for a puppy or a kitten. It had round ears and not pointed ones, a round little head which looked nothing like the face and the long pointed nose you find in an adult fox; its eyes were open. It had short fat legs, a short tail and was dark chocolate-brown in colour, not rusty-brown like an adult. Its coat was thick with mud and its right back leg had been bleeding. It smelt very foxy – foxes have a scent all of their own.

'Do you know what it is?' asked John.

'A fox cub,' I replied confidently.

'Hm. I thought you would know,' he said. 'How old do you think it is?' he asked.

'Well, the eyes are open and I think they open at about ten days. So it's probably only about twelve days old,' I said.

'Really,' was his reply.

'It's nearly dead,' I said touching the cub lightly with my finger.

'Yes, but it's just breathing,' he said hopefully.

'Only just. What do you want me to do with it?' I asked.

'Save it, Sir.'

'I don't know about that,' I replied. I wondered firstly whether I could save it, and secondly – would it be kinder to put it out of its misery.

'How did you get it?' I asked John.

He pulled up a chair and sat down. He was obviously going to tell me a story, but I must admit I was not prepared for the harrowing tale that followed.

'Well, Sir. I found it last evening about 5 pm. I came home from school and went for a walk across Bert Higgins' fields. As I reached the large wood on the far side of the farm I could see a pick-up truck parked at the side – next to that old fox's earth. I sneaked in the ditch along the side of the hedge slowly and silently – like a commando, Sir.'

'Go on,' I said.

'I knew that if Bert saw me he would chase me off. I got as close as I dare and then I just sat in the ditch and watched. Bert and his farm worker were digging at the earth. I saw them send the Jack Russell terriers

142

Vicky

down two holes; one terrier soon located the fox. I could hear the terrier barking underground. The two men dug down directly above the terrier; suddenly the fox bolted out of a hole and Bert's worker shot it.

'Was it killed?' I asked.

'No, it was only wounded. He shot it again, but it still didn't die. The two men ran after it, shot it again and brought the dead fox back and threw it in the back of the pick-up.'

I exhaled a deep breath. 'That seems like a horrible death,' I said.

'Yes Sir. It was awful.'

'So what happened next?' I asked.

'I could see the terriers playing with some dead cubs they had killed. The men then drove off in the pick-up. They didn't know that I had watched them.

'After they had left I walked over to the earth; I would have liked a fox's brush to hang on my bedroom wall and I thought there might have been a slim chance that another fox was killed before I arrived and maybe they had left it. There was no dead adult fox – so I didn't get my brush. I found three dead cubs but I didn't want their tails. Then I thought I heard a noise – a slight movement underground – it was down the hole where the men had been digging. I looked from the top but couldn't see anything. Then I got down on my hands and knees and put my arm down the hole. I was a bit worried because I couldn't see where I was putting my fingers – then I felt something furry – and I was sure it was a fox cub. I brought it out into the daylight. Its coat was muddy where the soil had caved in on it and its leg was cut.'

'This is quite a drama story,' I said. I was somewhat

143

disgusted at the clumsiness of the two men but I was very interested in John's side of the story. It was better than listening to one of Mr Beech's assemblies. Secretly I thought what a fascinating assembly it would make.

'What did you do next?' I asked.

'Well, I didn't take it to Bert – he would have told me off for being on his land and he would have killed the cub. I put it in my pocket. It was a great feeling – I could feel its little claws; it was moving towards my body – for warmth I suppose. I took it home but hadn't the courage to tell my mum and dad.'

'Why is that?' I asked.

'My dad would have knocked it at the back of the head with a shovel – he says foxes are vermin.'

'They are vermin,' I replied. 'So then what?'

'I smuggled it up to my bedroom and kept it in this shoe box under my bed.'

'Have you fed it?' I asked.

'I gave it some milk in a little dish and left it – but it didn't drink any. I then put some dog food in a dish but it wouldn't eat that either.'

'So what has it had to eat in the last sixteen hours?'

'Nothing really, except a few drops of milk that I squeezed into its mouth with a bit of sponge.'

'You mean, that's all it's had?' I said.

'Yes Sir,' he said guiltily.

'No wonder it's poorly. It's starving to death and it's cold,' I said, running my fingers along its back.

'Well it would be dead now if it wasn't for me,' he protested.

'You're right,' I said. 'I'm fed up with calling it "it",' I added. I picked the little thing up and turned it upside down 'It's a vixen.' I declared.

By this time assembly was over and a class of third-year pupils had come into the classroom. Some had ventured out to the front to look, others were sitting at their desks and craning their necks to see.

'Perhaps the kindest thing to do is put her out of her misery,' I suggested. They were appalled.

'Oh no, Sir,' said John, with a pitiful voice.

'You can't kill her, Sir,' said another girl.

Suddenly the whole class was against me. I felt I had better do something at least to try to save her or there would be a lynching party at four o'clock. It was clear they were not going to stand by and let me put her down. Inwardly I was delighted that they should care. It had been a good test of their true feelings towards animals. I really wanted to have a go at rearing her.

'Let's feed her and get her warm straight away, then,' I said.

'She'll live – won't she Sir?' asked John.

'She's got a slight chance – if I can get some food into her. But don't expect me to perform miracles.'

That day our lesson started with a question. 'What sort of food do you think we should give her?'

A loud chorus of 'colostrum' came back at me. Good! They were thinking along the right lines.

Sarah, our goat, had kidded only the day before, so she had plenty of colostrum. She was rearing two kids but she had far too much for them and some had been milked out that morning; in fact, it was still in the milking bucket. Colostrum is important for all mammals and they should drink it for the first three or four days of their lives. It protects the baby animals against common diseases and also contains vitamins and protein.

The colostrum started to go cold so I put a very small amount in a saucepan and warmed it on the boiler until it reached blood heat. If it had been a lamb that could not drink I would have placed a rubber tube down its throat into the stomach and poured some colostrum down, being careful to avoid the lamb's lungs. This fox cub was too small for me to do that. I had to do something quickly, so I took a small sterile syringe and filled it with colostrum. I opened her mouth with my finger and thumb and slowly squirted some colostrum into her, giving her only about a teaspoonful.

'She's certainly swallowed it,' I said.

'Good – perhaps we will rear her then,' said John.

'Don't count your chickens before they have hatched,' shouted Rachel.

'I'm not a pessimist,' said John, then continued: 'How often will she want feeding?'

'Every two or three hours,' I replied. I rubbed some antiseptic cream on her leg. She was shivering with cold, so I found a large cardboard box and placed a piece of blanket in the bottom; I put her on the blanket and covered her up with an old towel, and I placed the box next to the boiler in the classroom. Then I plugged in an infra-red lamp and hung this over her box. I had now done all that I could and she was soon asleep. But I wondered whether she would wake up. She stood a small chance of survival. Her future had still got to be decided, though. What could we do with her?

John ran off to his lesson; he was very late, but he

had a most original excuse. I bet no one had tried that one before. I also wondered what Mr Beech's reaction would be when I explained why I had missed the whole of his assembly.

At morning break I quickly drove to see Richard Jonas's mother. She had bred and exhibited Jack Russell Terriers for years and I knew that she sometimes hand-reared a pup, so she would be just the person to advise me.

The first thing she told me I needed was a premature puppy feeding bottle – a very small glass bottle with a tiny teat at the end. I told her that I had very little time, so she lent me one. She suggested that I reared the cub on substitute puppy milk which I could purchase from the vet's, or on goat's milk. She thought a teaspoonful of milk every two hours would be ideal.

I took the bottle back to school, sterilised it and then woke the cub up at 11.30 am. She was certainly more lively. She would not suck the teat on the bottle so I had to squeeze the teat gently into her mouth. She again swallowed about a teaspoonful.

I repeated the process at 1.30 pm. During the afternoon she became lively and started to scramble around her box – it was looking good, the combination of Sarah's colostrum and the warmth had brought her away from death's door. I took her home at teatime, put her box next to the boiler in the kitchen and hung her lamp above her.

At the 9.30 feed she began to suck the teat; she now knew what it was for, and it did not take her long to empty the small bottle. I set my alarm and got up every two hours in the night to feed her. At 7.30 in the morning I felt like a wrung-out dish cloth. I did not feel as though I had been to bed. And for most of the time I was in bed I did not sleep very well, for fear of over-sleeping for the next feed, or worrying about madam who slept soundly between each meal.

In the morning she was fine. I took her to school with me. The school is only a short distance away from where I live so it did not take long to get there.

John and about twenty of the other pupils were standing at the door of the classroom. They were all very eager to find out about her progress; they knew she was alive because they saw me carrying the box.

'Let me see – let me see,' they clamoured.

'She's doing fine,' I said. I felt like a Harley Street surgeon or Doctor Kildare talking about one of his patients.

I fed her again after she had settled down from her journey. John and the others were thrilled that she was actually sucking the teat. Her mouth was enormous for the size of her body and seemed out of proportion with the rest of her; she had a long tongue and she got better at drinking from the bottle at each feed.

After forty-eight hours I felt drained. She was drinking plain goat's milk now instead of colostrum, so she was being fed every three hours. Two-hourly feeds were killing me off. The three-hourly feeds were much more convenient, especially at night. It meant an 11 o'clock feed just before I went to bed, a 2 o'clock feed and a 5 o'clock feed. I only had to get up twice now instead of three times. This was a blessing because, oh boy, did I need some sleep!

Mrs Jonas told me to watch out in case the cub became constipated; in the wild the mother would lick the cub's backside to stimulate it and the cub would then go to the toilet. She seemed fine but I watched over her carefully.

'What are we going to call her?' I asked John.

'Vicky the Vixen,' he exclaimed, as if to imply, 'what else?'

'That's not very original,' I said.

'Can you come up with anything better then?' he said.

'I can't think of anything at the moment,' I admitted.

'Let's call her Vicky then, Sir?' he pleaded.

'All right, you win,' I capitulated.

After three days I was certain we would rear the cub. She slept a lot but she was now more active and she had put on a little weight.

'What are we going to do with her, Sir?' asked John.

'I have been waiting for you to ask me that,' I said seriously. 'It's obvious we can't let her go straight into the wild. She's not old enough to feed herself yet, she would be cold and hungry, and death within a day or two would be a certainty,' I said with authority.

'We could keep her for good, but that wouldn't be right, would it, Sir, keeping an animal in captivity on its own? Maybe we could find a wild-life park, sanctuary or zoo to take her in,' suggested John.

'Yes, but probably the best idea is to wait until she is older, then try releasing her. We would have to help her, though. Maybe let her go in a local wood, but take her food each day. We would have to gradually decrease the food to encourage her to catch her own.'

'That might be the best idea,' agreed John.

'There is a snag. She might become too tame and when released have too great a trust in man; she would probably even run up to a farmer for fuss or attention, and he would tell her to ''wait'' while he fetched his gun. There is also every chance she would get run over. So! What shall we do with her?'

'Try to let her go, but if she proves too tame then take her to a zoo.' I agreed with him.

I was now getting a lot of interest from my pupils. John wanted to be in charge of her, but there were many volunteers who wanted to help look after her. John agreed not to be greedy and share her with the others. He took charge of her and was not short of helpers.

In the daytime she was in the classroom where I taught the children – she was excellent 'live' material. Most of the pupils knew little or nothing about foxes so this was a first-class, close-up specimen.

'How big will she grow?' asked Rachel.

'About 35 cm high at the shoulder and about 60 cm long, with a tail – or brush as it is called – measuring about another 30 cm. But there are records of much larger foxes,' I said.

'What do they eat in the wild, Sir?' asked Paul.

'A lot of earthworms,' I replied.

That statement went down like a lead balloon. 'Oh Sir, you can't feed Vicky earthworms – they are horrible things,' said Paul.

'She's too young to eat them at the moment, but when she's older she may be given them. If we don't feed them to her she'll go foraging and find them for herself. They are a great delicacy to foxes,' I said.

'What else does she eat?' asked Julie.

150

'Rabbits, mice, field voles, pheasants, partridges, small birds, frogs, snails, insects, fruit and berries.'

'Oh, quite a gourmet then!' remarked Paul.

'How many litters does the mother fox have in one year?' asked Julie again.

'The vixen has only one litter with about four cubs,' I replied.

Vicky was the subject of various debates, some of them a bit heated. These included her future, fox hunting and shooting. She became stronger and did not need so much heat, so after she had been with us for one week I moved her box away from the boiler into another corner of the classroom.

I informed Mr Beech of our new arrival, unsure what his opinion of her would be. I told him the story and he was most impressed and sympathetic. He said he would pay her a visit as he had never seen a fox cub as young as this before. He came to see her that afternoon and approved of John's rescue operation. Mr Beech praised him for his courage and efforts and I could see John was very happy. Even so, I do not think Mr Beech appreciated the hard work I was putting in; it did not seem to register with him that I was getting up to feed her twice every night.

She seemed to be doing well. She was putting on weight and thriving on human company. My pupils could not get over her looks. She looked nothing like an elegant, sleek, sharp-nosed, red coloured fox; instead she was a stumpy, chocolate-brown, little dumpling, a bit like a corgi puppy that had been crossed with a kitten. Most baby animals are prettier when they are young and get less attractive when they are adult, especially piglets, lambs and calves. With a fox I think it is the other way around and I was looking forward to Vicky's sleek, sharp appearance as she got older.

At three weeks old she weighed one pound and ten ounces and she seemed to be doing well, I increased the amount of goat's milk at each feed, but cut her feeds down to one every four hours, which meant getting up just once in the night. I did not really like disturbing her and bringing her home every evening so I decided to keep her at school. She was now stronger and could walk about. I placed a large wire cage over the top of her box, so that she could go on walk-about and not stray. As each day went by she became more aware of us, and she started to get inquisitive.

She was now warm enough without her lamp. I replaced her box and cut a hole in the side of the new one for her to go in and out as she pleased. It was dark inside, she had her blanket in there and it was her own private place. She came out and walked around her large cage, but my pupils did not think that was enough.

'Can we give her a proper run in the classroom?' asked John.

'I don't see why not,' I said. We had just finished our lunch and it was a good opportunity. We shut the classroom door.

John lifted her out of her pen and put her on the classroom floor; she just lay there at first but after a few minutes she stood up and sniffed the floor. Then, very cautiously, she started to explore. She sniffed everything: tables, chair legs, cupboards and the sink unit. She was out for twenty minutes. We lifted her back into her pen, and after a few minutes she curled

152

up in her box and went fast asleep. Her new adventures had tired her out.

The next day, at lunchtime, the word had got out and John and I were surrounded by about twenty pupils – boys and girls of all ages – who wanted to see Vicky go for a walk. I said they could stay as long as they sat still, were quiet and did not frighten her.

Vicky was most obliging. Her second tour of the classroom was completed with a bit more confidence. Everyone in the room wanted to pick her up and cuddle her, but I stopped them as I wanted Vicky to explore. She smelled everyone's shoes. Suddenly Gillian moved her foot and Vicky scuttled back into her corner – she was frightened but she soon ventured out again.

One morning her feeding bottle leaked and the drops fell to the floor. She licked these up, so the next feed of milk was poured into a saucer. She just smelt it at first, but when I put my finger in it and then showed her my finger, she eagerly licked the milk off it. I dipped my finger back in the milk and she licked it again. She was quick to learn and started lapping the milk from the saucer. It was another step forward. A couple of days later I placed some puppy meal in the milk and very small pieces of chicken. She drank her milk first then started to investigate this new food which was soaked in milk. She did not sniff at it for long – she ate the lot. She was now almost four weeks old. She enjoyed her walks in the classroom and the pupils were now playing with her. She had teeth like needles and would playfully nip your fingers, but never hard enough to hurt. She would roll on her back and really enjoyed her games. I do not know who enjoyed the play most, Vicky or the pupils. She soon learned when she was coming out of her pen and would urinate in her excitement. She would hiss at us when annoyed. I introduced more and more solid food as each day went by.

At a month old she enjoyed a run on the lawn, where she would stop and dig the grass and then run around in excitement. She was now getting destructive; she would tear up paper and bite the legs of the chairs and tables. The pupils loved to have her out during lesson time. She liked to lie on their shoes and chew their shoe laces, pulling them undone and making them all wet and soggy. Her appearance was changing, especially her face. She was starting to get a long nose, her brush was getting thicker and her coat was changing to red in colour.

At two months all was going well until one morning she did not come out of her box for her feed. Diarrhoea was on the floor of her pen. John called her out. She did not move for a full minute, then she ventured out of her box into her run, looking very sorry for herself. She looked pitifully at her little stomach.

'We have been overfeeding her or she has got an infection,' I said to John.

'Are you going to give her an injection or medicine?' asked John.

'No. The vet can handle this one,' I said. 'If it was a sheep I would know what to do, but I've never treated a fox cub before.'

I told Mr Bell, the deputy headmaster, about our predicament, and I suggested that if he marked my register and I missed assembly I could take her straight away. John dashed off and told his form teacher that he was with me. I found another box – put Vicky in it and drove her to the vet's surgery.

We went straight in and Martin the vet was very surprised indeed to see me lift a young fox cub out of the box onto his table.

'This is a bit exotic, isn't it? When I saw you, John, I thought something was wrong with those prize Kerry Hill sheep of yours,' he said.

The veterinary nurse was also surprised. She ran to fetch another three nurses to have a look. After the 'Ah', 'Isn't she sweet?' and 'Oh bless her' had died down, the first of many questions was, 'Where did you get her from?'

Martin told me she had probably eaten too much. In fact the day before she did not have her usual brand of cat food because the shop had run out of supplies. I had bought another brand and the change of diet had upset her. He gave her a multivitamin injection, an antibiotic injection and handed me some tablets and medicine to give her to settle her stomach. I gave her only water and a little puppy meal for a couple of days before reintroducing meat. She soon got better, but needless to say we did not use that brand of cat food again.

She was now very active when she was out of her pen. She would jump onto chairs and get more mischievous each day. Her hearing was fantastic; she could hear someone walking across the playground before we did.

After her upset stomach we were careful to watch what we gave her and always introduced new foods

155

gradually. As well as the cat food, she also loved beef, chicken, chicken heads from Crawfords Poultry Farm, eggs, fruit and cooked vegetables. She was a greedy eater, often putting as much food in her mouth as possible before swallowing.

At four months old she had lost her little cub appearance. Her chocolate-brown had changed to red-brown; she looked like a small fox rather than a big cub, and she was very quick in her movements. However, she was too tame to let go – she trusted us and would not survive in the different life she would find in the wild. She had never had to catch her own prey.

She became more and more of a character, often jumping on to your lap for fuss. One day when John was with her in the classroom, she jumped on to his shoulders. 'Sir – look at her Sir,' exclaimed John with delight. She lay across his neck.

'You have got a fox fur stole on, John – but this time the fox is still wearing it as well,' I laughed.

John walked around and Vicky loved it. She grinned and felt very pleased with herself.

In lesson time she loved to come out and venture between the pupils' tables. She would play havoc, sneaking up to pupils' bags, putting her nose in and then pulling out writing books, textbooks, pens, pencils and rulers – often stealing them and taking them back into her box. She would often destroy her finds. Of course, my classes loved it. They thought a mischievous fox far more interesting to look at and play with than to listen to me teaching them. She practically shredded the doormat. If anyone made a sudden movement with their arm or leg she would often dash back to her own corner venturing out a few minutes later to sneak up on some poor unsuspecting pupils and give them the fright of their lives.

John gave her a ball of wool to play with. She got it everywhere. She ran around the classroom with it, getting it all knotted up around chair legs, table legs and pupils' legs. She got herself so securely tied up that the only way we could free her was with a pair of scissors.

She had a very pungent smell, a smell that was very difficult to get rid of. She was making the classroom 'hum' a bit: I was forever spraying the room with air freshener. Some pupils would make a fuss and complain 'It smells in here, Sir.' Others did not bother but I did not want any complaints to Mr Beech. I therefore built her a pen in the garden. I constructed this with 2 in × 2 in timber and stapled on weldmesh, and I made her a wooden kennel to sleep in. She slept inside there in the dark but I have often found her asleep out-side on top of the kennel. She would curl up in a ball with her brush covering her nose – she would soon wake up if she heard us.

Vicky recognised the scent of John or me, and she would urinate in excitement when she saw us. She would often play at 'killing' her food – pouncing on it like a cat and shaking it in her mouth like a terrier dog. She also liked to bury some, placing the food in a corner, piling soil on top with her nose and pressing the soil down hard with her nose.

It was now winter and Vicky had grown up into a large and beautiful animal – she was very sleek with not a whisker out of place.

John bought her a collar and lead so that he could take her on longer walks. John put the collar on her when she was playing, and at first she did not notice it. Then she realised – she sat down and tried to look at it over her shoulder. She did not like it and tried to scratch it off. She soon got used to it, though, and a couple of days later we attached the lead. She was hopeless. She kept rolling over to play and biting it, then she would run very fast and we would have to run with her; she would then suddenly stop.

'I don't think she will ever walk to heel,' I said.

'Can we take her out of the school?' asked John.

'I'm not too keen,' I said. 'She might get off the lead and run into the road.'

'No, Sir. She never gets off her lead,' John pleaded.

'She might be attacked by someone's dog – they are natural enemies, you know,' I said.

Vicky

'Well, what if two or three of us went to protect her?' he persisted. In the end I gave in and agreed. Guess who went with them. I did.

She was fine until the first car went by – she crouched down low and was frightened. The second car that came by nearly crashed. The driver and passenger looked at the fox, looked back at each other then looked at the fox again. So intent were they on watching our vixen they nearly crashed into a parked vehicle. People walking in the street stared in amazement, then gave a cry of delight and stooped to stroke her. But she did not act as she would have done in school. This was not her territory, and she was petrified. We did not take her out of the school gates again.

She enjoyed life at school but what was to become of her? She was a lovely animal and it would be criminal to let her go free. It was decision time – although we thought the world of her we decided to let her leave us.

We were sad to see her go, but she now lives happily in a sanctuary.

Mice and a Horrible Smell

'MR TERRY, Mrs Stephens, the supervisor of our kitchens, has reported to me today that there is a fieldmouse
in the school kitchens,' said Mr Beech.

'Oh? Well what's that got to do with me?' I asked.

'We think it might have come from the school
farm.'

'Why do you think that?' I enquired.

'Well, mice are attracted to foodstuffs, aren't they?'
he said.

'Yes, and that's probably why they are in the kitchens,' I replied.

'The caretaker has telephoned for the rodent officer
to call,' he said.

'Oh good,' I said, thinking to myself, 'it's nothing
to do with me.'

'Would you mind if the officer visited the farm

to make sure you haven't got a mouse problem?' he asked.

'He can come and look, but I don't think for one moment he will find any mice,' I answered. Trust the farm to get the blame, I thought.

It was probably not a fieldmouse at all. I would like to bet it was a common house mouse. The long-tailed fieldmouse prefers to live in fields and hedgerows rather than a school kitchen; its relative, the house mouse, is the one that likes the great indoors, making itself equally at home in houses, sheds and buildings. This creature originated from Asia and can now be found all over the world where people live, reaching many of those faraway places as stowaways on ships.

They are very active little creatures which will move very quickly back to their holes when alarmed; they are good at climbing and can even climb a brick wall. They can produce four or five litters of young in one year, with five or six or even more young born in each litter. I have often seen nests of mice. When born, the mice are naked and blind and look horrible, but after two weeks they can feed themselves, and after six weeks they could start breeding. Given this information, it is a good task to set the pupils a problem: 'If a pair of house mice set up home in the school kitchens on 1st January how many mice could be present on the 31st December?' Afterwards, the pupils hopefully tell me why we are not overrun with these mice, giving reasons such as deaths due to disease, overcrowding and cats and other predators, as well as poisoning and trapping.

Often pupils do not like the idea of poisoning or

trapping them. I do. I find them a real menace: they nibble open bags of animal food, the food falls out of the bags, they eat some of it and leave their droppings which our livestock could eat. Consequently I try to exterminate them.

We do occasionally get a few mice, but four or five of our neighbours own cats; the cats find it fun to spend most of the day and night on our farm. We have a shed where we keep straw; the cats often lie on the bales and look very disgruntled if we want to use the bale that has been their bed. Hay and straw will attract mice and rats, but if the cats get in the shed I find that they keep the rodent population at bay.

The school farm does not own a cat, we just leave it to the neighbourhood moggies to get on with the job. There is no doubt about it – they love their work. It is very interesting watching a cat stalking its prey. I was doing so one day when I asked Christopher Hutchinson to name four members of the cat family. 'The father cat, the mother cat and her kittens,' came the quick-witted reply. He was fast becoming the class comedian although he still was not up to Steven Wood's standard. Steven was one of the first pupils I ever taught, one of the original fifteen pupils who took rural studies back in 1974.

As I helped myself to lunch at our cafeteria system in our dining room, I could see Mrs Stephens hovering in the background – she was making sure her ladies were working.

'I hear there's a mouse in the kitchens,' I said.

Her face was a picture, showing every aspect of

possible alarm. Her eyes widened, her mouth opened but no sound came out. She ran over to me.

'Mr Terry, keep your voice down.' She then started to talk very quietly. 'We don't want the children to know. It only takes one of them to tell their parents and the kitchens may be closed down and my ladies would have to stop at home. The school might even have to close because we couldn't provide the dinners.'

'Well, if the school is going to close, I'll say it a bit louder,' I joked – but I think her sense of humour was having a day off. She could not see the funny side.

The next day I asked her quietly if she still had got the mouse.

'Yes, one of the ladies saw it run across the floor early this morning,' she said. 'I want to ask you a favour.'

'What's that?' I asked.

'To tell you the truth I've got a man coming from the Public Health department at 10 o'clock tomorrow morning to look at our conditions. The Rodent Officer has not been and I'm worried that when the health person calls he might see a mouse run across the floor – it could close the kitchens,' she said.

'I know, and it could even close the school,' I said in fun. 'So what's the favour?'

'Please come and find the mouse, catch it and get rid of it,' she said. Who did she think I was? The pied piper of Warwickshire?

'Can't you get your ladies to do it?' I asked.

'No, we don't like mice. I hate to see them run, and the bare tail gives me the creeps,' she replied.

'Couldn't Mr Beech help you?' I asked, grasping at straws.

'No, Mr Terry. He is the headmaster and I don't think he would take too kindly to mouse catching,' she said.

'Can't you make a noise like a piece of cheese?' I asked.

'Don't be silly, Mr Terry,' she said.

'I'll try – I'll come around to the kitchens at 4 o'clock,' I assured her.

'I don't want you to kill it, though. I want you to catch it alive and then let it go,' she said in a very concerned voice.

'All right, I'll do my best,' I said.

I went to meet her at 4 pm with two of my second-year pupils, named John and Paul. I had rarely seen the kitchens from the other side, and my heart sank when I saw the size of the cupboards. It was going to be a mammoth task searching those huge things for one little mouse.

'Where did you last see it?' I asked.

'It ran into that cupboard over there,' she said.

She pointed to one of the biggest cupboards. I opened the door to reveal saucepans of all sizes. John, Paul and I started to empty the cupboard, putting all the saucepans on the floor – but we found no mouse or indeed any evidence of it. John and Paul started to put everything back. The next cupboard was the same size; this also contained saucepans, but still no mouse. The next cupboard was in a corner.

I moved some jars and containers and out shot the mouse, running towards Mrs Stephens. 'Oh, it's coming towards me,' she screamed.

164

'Watch out, Miss. It will run up your leg,' shouted John at the top of his voice.

'Get it away from me,' she shrieked.

With her screaming, the poor frightened thing ran out of the door on to the playground.

'Thank you Mr Terry,' she said.

'That's got rid of it,' said Paul.

'Thank you so much Mr Terry,' she said again.

'I expect it will find its way to the farm and find a nice warm new home to snuggle into,' said John.

'I hope so,' said Mrs Stephens. 'I don't want it back.'

John was probably right; we would no doubt inherit it.

The next day the public health inspector came and the kitchens easily passed all the regulations – it was of course, due to a little help from John, Paul and me. During the afternoon the rodent officer called at the kitchens and put down some poison in case the mouse had some companions. He then called to see me. He was a good, helpful man called Mr Hawkins, and seemed impressed with the farm. We keep our bags of feedstuff in a brick foodstore which is kept shut and locked to keep out vermin. In our large wooden shed the foodstuffs are kept in half a dozen plastic food bins – all with their lids on. Again, this minimises rodent infestations.

'If you get any mice or rats, give me a ring. Don't buy any poison, Warwickshire County Council are paying for this service,' he said.

I thanked him and told him I would remember what he said.

A couple of days later I asked Mrs Stephens if she

had seen any more mice. She had not, and neither had any of her ladies; so that little drama was over.

During January I saw a couple of mice behind our rabbit cages in our wooden building. I moved the cages and found a small hole in the concrete floor, and next to it a pile of soil – our visitors had been excavating.

I telephoned Warwickshire County Council who said they would send out the rodent officer. I waited for over a week, and the way mice breed that was a long time. I had visions of being overrun by them. I

was beginning to wonder if it would have been better just to buy some poison, but Mr Hawkins had said to call him out.

I was teaching the fifth years – the topic was clay soil and sandy soil – when I saw an attractive lady walking towards the classroom. She was blonde, about twenty-four years old, wearing a tight white T-shirt, a short denim skirt and white high-heeled shoes. Some of the lads had spotted her as well and some ribald comments issued forth. She knocked on the classroom door and walked in. The fifth year boys were openly ogling.

'Good morning, are you Mr Terry?' she asked.

'I am,' I replied.

'I'm Miss Ashton. Warwickshire County Council have called me out to look at your mice problem.'

'Oh well, you are the prettiest rodent officer I ever saw,' I said, meaning it to be a compliment. However, she did not take it the way it was meant.

'Maybe, but please don't talk to me that way,' she said, snootily.

'That's put me in my place,' I thought.

'I'm not actually the rodent officer – Mr Hawkins left rather suddenly and I'm doing this job as a sort of stand-in,' she explained.

'I'll show you where the mice are,' I offered.

She pulled a face and walked outside with me. I showed her the rabbit cages. 'I wouldn't say it was a big mouse, but it's set a trap for me,' I joked. She was not amused and just screwed her nose up. 'I'll move the cages and you can see the hole,' I continued.

'That will not be necessary,' she said. She went to the car and brought back a small cardboard box with a hole at each end and a bag of poison. She put some poison in the box, carefully handling it with rubber gloves on. 'There you are,' she said. 'You will have to put it behind the cages, Mr Terry, because if I see a mouse run I will die. I'm scared stiff of them.'

'You are joking.' I said.

'No, really I'm scared of them. I have to admit it.'

'I'll put it behind the hutches if it makes you feel better,' I said. 'Can I have some more poison please and I will refill the box when they have eaten it?'

'No. I'll come back with some more.'

'I'll keep it under lock and key,' I promised.

'No – it's more than my job's worth,' she said.

'Do you think you will keep this job long?' I asked. She did not answer.

'Yes', I ploughed on, 'if you are doing this job for some time you will surely see mice and big rats. Rats as big as cats.' The venom shot from her eyes.

'Don't mention rats', she snarled. 'I'm petrified of them as well.' I thought it was time I kept quiet; I was definitely beginning to annoy her.

By this time some of my fifth-year lads had wandered outside on the pretext of looking at the animals. Anthony and Ian, two rather untrustworthy lads, were trying to listen to our conversation but were pretending to take a great interest in Sarah our goat.

Suddenly the likely lads dashed behind a feed bin.

'Here it is. Here, look,' yelled Anthony excitedly. 'I've got it, I've got it.' He picked something up. I could not see what it was but it looked furry. Then he threw it in Miss Ashton's face. 'It's a mouse – a mouse,' he shouted. It hit her full in the face. Miss Ashton

168

Mice and a Horrible Smell

screamed at the top of her voice, dropped the bag of
poison and ran like the wind out of the shed onto the
playground. The boys laughed gleefully.

The 'mouse' which had fallen to the floor was
nothing more than a lamb's tail.

'You stupid pair of idiots,' I shouted at them. I
ran after Miss Ashton who by this time had reached
her car, and already had the engine turning. The car
roared into life, the tyres screeched and doing a fair
imitation of Nigel Mansell she was soon out of sight.

The two lads walked sheepishly back into the classroom. The full impact of their foolish act had hit
home – the others in the class asked them what
was going on and why had she driven away so
fast.

'What did you throw that lamb's tail in her face for?'
I demanded.

'It was only a joke, Sir,' said Anthony. 'We didn't
mean any harm.'

'I don't suppose you did – but this time I think you
have picked on the wrong lady,' I said.

'You mean she was a drip, Sir?' smirked Ian.

'No, I do not mean she was a drip. I mean that I
don't think you two have heard the last of this,' I said.
That wiped the smile off his face.

'Do you think she will report us to the headmaster,
Sir?' asked Ian.

'I wouldn't be a bit surprised if it went even higher,'
I said.

'Oh no, Sir,' they both groaned.

'Oh yes, Sir,' I mimicked. 'So you'd better tell me
what you intend to do about it.'

'A letter of apology . . .,' suggested Ian.

Ducks in Detention

'Might be a good idea,' I said. 'The best one you've had all day – but you are not writing it in my class. You can stay in and do it at break time.'

'Oh Sir,' they protested.

'You are staying in, and that's it,' I persisted.

Anthony's English was poor but Ian's was above average so it was Ian who dictated what went in to the letter in the long run. But Ian was not going to 'carry the can' on his own, and made Anthony make some suggestions. They worked well together, and all I had to do when they showed me the letter was to insert a few commas and correct the spelling of the word 'apology'.

'Is it good enough?' asked Ian.

'Yes, but copy it out again – it needs to be neater,' I said.

'Oh Sir, it's nearly the end of break,' said Anthony, pulling a face and pointing to his watch.

'Well that's too bad, isn't it? You'll just have to come back at afternoon break and finish it,' I said.

'Oh Sir!'

'No arguing – you will come back,' I ordered.

The lads did come back. Ian made a neat copy and addressed the envelope. They now just needed to buy a stamp and post it on the way home.

'We will keep this copy in case Mr Beech does find out and wants to read it,' suggested Ian.

'Good idea,' agreed Anthony.

'If we have another mouse problem do you think Miss Ashton will come out to this school to help us again?' I asked.

'It's doubtful, Sir – but she might if she reads this letter and accepts our apology,' said Ian.

Mice and a Horrible Smell

'I hope so,' I replied, but I knew she would not be back. Never mind, at least I had gained the bag of poison that she had dropped.

The next morning I got the royal command. A note in my pigeon hole said *Please see me regarding the mouse lady*. It was signed, *Mr Beech*.

I want to see him straight after assembly. It was fortunate for me he had given a good assembly and was feeling very pleased with himself; now was the time to see him.

'Now, Mr Terry. I've received this letter this morning from the acting rodent officer – a Miss Ashton. She claims that a boy from this school threw a dead mouse in her face. Is that so?' He paused, then said in his sternest voice, 'I am appalled that such a thing should happen in my school. Can you explain?'

I could, and I did. 'Well, it was like this, headmaster . . .' and I told him the whole story.

'Send the lads to me,' he said. I located the boys, Anthony in a physics lesson and Ian in chemistry. They both went to see Mr Beech at morning break and came back looking very crestfallen. They had taken the letter with them and Mr Beech had been impressed with it. Their behaviour, however, had made a very different impression on him. He made them miss all of their morning and afternoon breaks for a week – indeed, for the duration of those times they had to stand outside the staffroom.

'Serves you jolly well right,' I said. 'Perhaps in future you will stop to think about the consequences of your actions.'

The boys did not receive a reply from Miss Ashton. I could not help wondering if she gave up her job as a temporary rodent officer on the day she had had a little lamb's tail thrown in her face.

We did not need the services of a rodent officer until twelve months later and then another man came out, a Mr Farmer. He was certainly not scared of mice. I nearly asked him what had happened to Miss Ashton but decided against it. Let sleeping dogs lie is my motto.

I seem to see mice more in the winter months than the summer. However, one hot summer we did have a problem. It wasn't mice this time though, it was a horrible smell in the school – and at the time it seemed worse than any problems we ever had with mice. It was dreadful.

One hot July afternoon, Mr Beech called me to his office.

'Mr Terry, there's an awful smell in the corridor, in the part of the school next to the staffroom, and at the rear of the school next to the farm.'

'Is there really, headmaster?' I replied, thinking to myself here we go again.

'I didn't want to ask you in front of the others, but have you been mucking out the livestock, and has some of the smell from the manure drifted into the school?'

I knew it. I knew we would get the blame. Before I could answer, he went on, 'You can't be too careful you know. I wouldn't want someone branding you a health hazard.'

Well, I've been called some things in my time – but never a health hazard.

'No, headmaster, we have not been mucking out the livestock. I walked through the corridors earlier this afternoon and I didn't smell anything,' I said.

'Well, no disrespect, man – but you wouldn't notice it would you. I think over the years you have become immune to all smells.'

'I wouldn't say that,' I replied.

'You seem as happy as a pig in it,' he said seriously.

'Well it's not the farm,' I assured him.

Trust the farm to get the blame again – we get the blame for everything from mice in the kitchens to running up the national debt. What next?

The next morning, as always, I went into the staff-room to check the notice board and see if there were any messages in my pigeon-hole. I was greeted with the words, 'It smells again this morning in here. Have you been mucking out?' This was Mr Petty.

'No we haven't. Mr Beech has already asked me the same question,' I replied.

Mr Searle came in, turned up his nose and said, 'What's that awful smell?'

'It don't half pen and ink,' said Mr Smyth in his broad Cockney accent.

'Well, I can assure you it most certainly is not the farm,' I said, stating my case positively.

From my mobile classroom set across the play-ground I have a good view of the school and play-ground, and at about ten o'clock I could see the caretaker checking all the drains on the playground. He was thrusting drain rods down, and yards of them were disappearing. All the manhole covers were up. It looked as if the smell could be a blocked drain. Pupils were walking around the school holding their noses or screwing up their faces in distaste. At lunchtime I saw the caretaker.

'Have you sorted the problem out yet?' I asked him.

'No. They don't seem blocked to me. Mr Beech has called the experts in, they will check the whole drainage system tomorrow.' The next day officials from Warwickshire County Council arrived. They were dressed in suits and carried plans of the drains, so they were advisors and not the manual workers. A little later two workers arrived in a green Ford van – they soon got to work and spent the whole day pushing the rods through the drains.

I ventured into the staffroom. Mr Martin, the head of Maths, said, 'I still think it's the farm. It smells rotten – like a dead goat or sheep. With this roasting weather the smell has drifted this way.'

'It is not the farm,' I persisted. 'We haven't had a bereavement and our buildings are spotlessly clean.'

'Perhaps someone's committed a murder and there's a body rotting under the floorboards,' suggested Mr Petty. What sort of reading material did he indulge in?

I could smell it. It was getting worse with each hour that passed. It seemed worse to me actually in the staffroom itself. But where the devil was it coming from?

Mr Beech pinned a notice to the notice board stating that the workers had found nothing wrong with the drains.

The sun continued to beat down, the temperatures reached ninety, the ground was bone dry and we desperately needed rain.

The caretaker cleaned out the large rubbish bins at

Mice and a Horrible Smell

the rear of the school and disinfected them, and he did the same with the small dustbins. The school kitchen then came under close scrutiny – there was nothing wrong.

'It's nice to come down to the farm, Sir. It smells better than the school,' said Fiona Westwood, a third-year pupil who did not usually enjoy farmwork, because of the smells. One pupil had complained to his parents about the obnoxious smell and a concerned mother had telephoned the school.

On Friday another team of workers came, this time to check the sewer from the toilets which lead into the pipes across the playground, and then into the main sewerage system under the road. From my window I saw Mr Beech walk smartly and briskly up to the workers. He had a clipboard in his hand and looked very official. I could see the workers shaking their heads, and then Mr Beech shook his head. The mystery remained.

'Will the school have to close down?' asked Fiona, hopefully.

'I very much doubt it – I'm sure someone will find the cause of this smell soon,' I replied.

However, the experts had still not come up with the answer.

At break time the following Tuesday, Mr Martin sat as usual in the staffroom talking with a group of staff, including me. He suddenly said, 'What's this plastic bag doing under this chair?' and at the same time slid out the bag and carefully opened the top. He recoiled in horror and, grimacing, said, 'that's rotting flesh.'

The room went silent as we all looked at Mr Martin. 'It's disgusting, take a look at that. Is it some of your lot playing about?' he asked me.

I looked inside the bag and the stench made my eyes water. 'Oh crikey, dear me no. Nothing to do with us,' I said. Inside the bag the rotting flesh was riddled with maggots.

'I said the other day that it smelled like rotting flesh,' he said, holding the bag at arm's length.

Just then, Mr Pointer looked up. 'I had forgotten all about that,' he said. All eyes turned accusingly on him. He went bright red. 'I'm awfully sorry. David Jones in the fifth year, whose father is a butcher, brought me some pigs' lungs to dissect in biology. He brought them to me at coffee time. I thanked him, sat to finish my coffee and forgot all about them. . . .'

'Well, they're pretty ripe now – look at them,' said Mr Martin, in anger. 'Go on, take them, I don't want the blessed things. The stench is enough to kill you,' he said, prodding the bag towards Mr Pointer.

'How long ago did David give you the lungs?' I asked suspiciously.

'About a month ago,' he replied sheepishly.

'Gordon Bennett,' said Mr Martin. 'It's a wonder the damn things didn't walk out of here on their own and come looking for you.'

Mr Pointer gingerly took hold of the bag and started to walk towards the door.

'What are you going to do now?' asked Mr Petty. 'Dissect the maggots?'

Mr Pointer did not answer, he was too embarrassed.

During the next lesson, two lads came to my classroom with a request.

'Could Mr Pointer borrow a spade, please – we have got to dig a very large hole for him,' asked one of the lads.

'It's a pleasure!' I said, handing out two spades.

The smells were going to be laid to rest. Thus ended another drama at our school.

A New Extension and a
Worrying Twenty Minutes

ONE OF my ex-pupils – Daniel – had offered to come and help build an extension on to our large wooden building. It was good that a former pupil was still interested; after all, he had left school and was working for a local builder, so it did not really matter to him.

But he had always been keen to lend a hand and got stuck in to whatever task I gave him without standing about talking, or hindering in any way. I will always remember Daniel for one particular incident at school (recorded in *Pigs in the Playground*). That was the day he cleaned out the calves and his hands were covered in calf muck which had stuck on. Then, without washing his hands, he sat and calmly ate a pound of strawberries. After eating the fruit his hands were still caked in the brown stuff, but he had the cleanest fingertips in the whole school. Do you know, the lad never had a day's illness in his life!

It would mean some hard work from both of us and from some of my pupils – I was confident some would volunteer to help. Next year we would have even more ewes to lamb at school and we could certainly now do with the extra space at lambing time – space had been tight the previous spring. All our ewes are in-wintered in January until they lamb in March; once lambing begins, space gets tighter and tighter. Once the ewes have lambed they are put in mothering-up pens which are small pens made out of hurdles, where the mother can get used to her lambs and vice-versa. After a few days they are taken out of the mothering-up pens and ewes and lambs run together in groups – coming indoors for the night until April or May.

It was the autumn term, so it would be good to get the building up before we housed the ewes in January and before the inclement weather started; we could also work after school until darkness fell. Daniel would help after he finished work in the evenings and at weekends.

Our existing timber building was an excellent dual-purpose shed. We had built the first three bays over a period of three years, building one bay each year. Each bay measures 12 feet by 24 feet. A fourth bay, 15 feet by 24 feet, was added in 1981. The four bays all joined together made a building that was 24 feet by 51 feet. We had constructed a walk-through feeding passage three feet wide and running the length of the building, and this was made from galvanised gated hurdles. In each bay one hurdle had a gate built into it which enabled anyone to walk into that section.

The shed itself was built by making wooden frames out of 2 inch square timber and the matchboarding was nailed on. The upright posts were concreted into the ground, and all the sections were bolted together.

I made some drawings. I wanted the largest building possible. We could not extend the building at the front because it was close to the mobile classrooms. We could not extend at the rear because it was near the neighbours' back gardens. On the near side was a path which led to our vegetable garden and on the left of the path was a large heather garden. I did not want to disturb the path or the heathers. The obvious place to fit an extension was on the far side. It could not run the whole 51 feet of the building because of another neighbour's back garden hedge, but we could make it 27 feet long, and we would be able to extend outwards for 15 feet.

I wanted the extension to look the same as the other building. This new extension I would divide into two, making a wooden gate to get into the far side. I telephoned Daniel and he came to school the next evening to have a look at my plans. He liked them.

'Order all the materials, get the foundations dug out and put the rubble in the excavations for the base, and I'll be back for some skilled work,' he said.

I measured it and worked out what we would need. I telephoned our local building supplier and I spoke to Garry, one of my former pupils who now had a good job with them. Garry gave me a very good discount indeed. 'My boss will shoot me,' he said. Everything could be purchased from this firm except the roofing sheets and the electrical wiring switches and lights.

I marked out the proposed area with a fourth-year class in tow, knocking in stakes at the corners and running string from the pegs. It was a large job to dig out the topsoil – some volunteer pupils did some during lesson time but most of it was done after school and at weekends. We spread this topsoil over our vegetable and flower garden. In the end, the excavations were eight inches deep; we would put rubble in this and then sand, ready to take a paving slab floor.

I had no rubble or hardcore and I asked my pupils at

the start of each lesson if any of them had any rubble in their back gardens. One lad did bring in a wheelbarrowful but that did not go very far. I telephoned Daniel and told him I was having difficulty finding any; he would ask his boss, but he was not very hopeful. At 5.30 the next day Daniel did appear with a wheelbarrowful from his own back garden. He did two more trips, but of course we still did not have enough. I then had the idea of driving around the district to look for a rubbish skip – perhaps someone in the area was knocking down a wall in their house or carrying out some building work.

I found a skip parked in Warwick Road. It was piled high with rubble and an old door frame, and I could see that the garage had been knocked down. I rang the doorbell.

A tall, thin man aged about forty answered the door.

'Hello, I'm John Terry – ' I said. But before I could say anything else he replied, 'I know. You're a teacher at the school.'

'That's correct,' I answered.

'You're not scrounging, are you?' he asked.

'Well – in a way I suppose I am,' I said. He had obviously heard about me.

'My son is in one of your rural studies classes, and he comes home trying to sell us eggs, oven-ready chickens, half-pigs for the freezer, vegetables and fruit.'

'I expect he does,' I said. 'Who is your son?'

'Julian Green,' he said.

'Oh yes, a good lad. He does sell a lot of produce.'

'I'm the mug who buys most of it,' he joked. 'What can I do for you?'

181

'I want some rubble, and I can see you have got a whole skip full parked out in the road. I want some for the base of our new shed extension.'

'Help yourself,' he said. 'But you'd better get a move on because the firm that owns the skip will be calling for it tomorrow.'

'Thanks very much,' I said. I was very pleased.

I returned home and telephoned Daniel. He was not busy and could help me collect the rubble out of the skip that evening; outside the local shops I spotted two of my fifth-year lads – both big and strong. I persuaded them to come and help us as well, they were not doing anything except sitting on the bench watching the girls go by.

I hitched up our livestock trailer and waited for my three helpers to arrive – the lads had gone home to get changed. I had the feeling they were grateful for the chance of something to do. We were soon in Warwick Road. We were careful not to overload the trailer – we unloaded the rubble on the edge of the playground and as near to the new building as I could get. We did another two loads, but by that time it was getting dark and we all felt we had worked hard enough.

The next day my pupils loaded the old bricks up in wheelbarrows and tipped them in the excavations. We had enough and it certainly made a good hard foundation for the building. I had ordered fifteen scoops of sand from Garry for sixty pounds. This came the next day and was also tipped on the playground. Once again my pupils got down to wielding their shovels and loading wheelbarrows, and tipped it on top of the rubble, about three inches deep. There was too much sand. We had estimated it well because we

182

would need some more to mix with cement and some to lay slabs on around the outside of the building.

We bought eighty paving slabs to slab the shed floor and for the path to go at the front, rear and side of the building. Once the sand was in position I telephoned Daniel for him to come and help with the slab laying. I was getting the sand really level when he arrived. I should have known he would have something to say, and I was right.

'Playing in the sand then are we?' he said smugly.

'Yes,' I said with a sigh. 'It's the nearest I'll get to a beach for a while.'

It was 5.30 pm. 'I'm ready to make a start,' said Daniel.

'Well, I'm going home for my tea,' I said.

'Don't be long then,' he said eagerly.

'I'll be twenty minutes,' I replied.

We are now good at slab laying. I have put down about eight hundred at the school. Most of them are the large ones measuring three feet by two feet. They take some handling as well. Daniel and I made a good team, and with the aid of a spirit level we laid ten slabs on that first evening. Daniel used his weight to jump on the slabs to get them exactly right. The second evening we laid twelve. It took nine days (or rather, evenings) to complete the job.

We built the shed after school and at weekends. It is difficult for me to do much during lesson time because if I take a class of pupils out, I can not find enough jobs for thirty of them to work on. It is skilled work, so I like to give it my full concentration.

The sides were constructed the same as our existing building. We bolted it on to this and made a doorway from the old building through to the new one. Once again we made the doors and we also put a dividing wall in the building, making and fixing a wooden gate to separate one part from the other part.

After fixing the roof and the gutterings we creosoted the sides of the building and then painted the doors blue to match the blue doors on the existing building. However, they made the old doors look shabby, so we finished up painting all of them. We had a professional electrician in to fix some fluorescent lights (that's a thought – could I persuade one of my pupils to become an electrician, I wondered). The last job was laying the paving slabs around its perimeter. All of this went very smoothly and we had no real problems.

I was very pleased when it was all finished – it was very hard work and we had completed it in six weeks. The total cost was £933.21. Of course there were no labour charges, the services of Daniel and me were voluntary, and so too was the help of many pupils. It looked the same as the existing building and even Mr Beech said it looked splendid. Our bank balance had been severely hit and we were down to about ten pounds. I now had to start the hard sell and get my pupils to buy oven-ready chickens, using the profits to build the bank balance up again.

Our building work was completed well within the time limits – it was the end of October and we did not need it until the following January when it would be used for housing our in-lamb ewes.

The ewes were living with the ram, Randy Dandy, about ten miles away on some grass keep we rent each autumn on a dairy farm. The grass was usually plentiful but this time it was not growing as well as usual, and the sheep really needed a change. I mentioned this to Richard Jonas.

'They can graze one of our fields for a month,' he said, 'and then they can go back. It will do our field good; it's had dairy cows on it during the summer, but there's no end of grass on it now and the frost will only kill it.'

'Thanks very much – that will be most helpful,' I said. 'If the frost is going to kill it and our sheep will do your field good, does that mean they can come rent free?' I asked.

'Certainly not,' he said. 'It will be the going rate: twenty pence per week per sheep.' I agreed, and the next evening after school I took Susan and Michael to fence it in with electric netting. The field was situated on the side of the busy A5. It was fenced well enough for cattle but it was not good enough for sheep, there were many holes in the hedge and I did not want any of the sheep creeping through onto the busy road.

Susan, Michael and I work well as a team and we soon used up eleven rolls of electric netting, standing it up around the edge of the field. The power came from a small electric fencer unit with a 6 volt battery, and once the sheep get a shock or two they soon learn to stay away from the fence. There was a water trough in the field but it was too high up for the sheep to reach so we filled some buckets and left them for the flock to drink out of. We finished off just before it got dark.

Michael and Susan came with me the next afternoon to fetch the sheep from the farm. I had two free periods and was able to sneak out of school with

these two enthusiastic pupils. The sheep were easily driven out of their field; they were bored and wanted a change. We put them into a pen in the corner of the farmyard and wormed them. Randy Dandy had marked all twenty-four of them with the coloured crayon that he wears in his harness. This is called a raddle mark, and when he mates with them he leaves a mark on their backs. We can then count 147 days after the mark and we then have some idea of the lambing date. Some sheep come on heat sixteen to seventeen days after being served which means they are not in lamb. We change the colour of the crayon, and if a ewe is served again we calculate the new lambing date.

We wormed all the ewes and Randy Dandy, and loaded half of them in the trailer. We took them in two loads but even with the decks in the trailer it would have been a very tight squeeze to get them all in.

Once in the new field the sheep put their heads down and grazed and grazed for all they were worth. They would do well here as it had not supported sheep for a number of years.

I walked all the way round the perimeter of the field to check the electric fence. It was fine, we had made a first-class job of putting it up. The fence was working and I would sleep well, knowing the sheep were safe.

Richard Jonas's father told me two or three farmers who were passing by asked if he had started to keep sheep. Not likely, he had told them. A few farmers asked me if they were ours, most of them guessing or realising they were. Actually they looked lovely from the road, their black-and-white markings looking very distinctive. I wondered how many ordinary travellers along that road would notice them as they passed by.

I saw Matt Corbutt in the Black Horse one evening.

'Your sheep look well in that field next to the A5, but I hope you're keeping it secure because I would hate them to get out and cause a nasty accident, especially if it was at night. It would be quite a pile-up, you know.'

'I agree, Matt. I did worry before I put them in the field, but I've fenced it with electric netting. It's a new fencer unit and battery and it gives quite a kick, so they won't get out.'

'I don't want to worry you, but I had an electric fencer unit stolen last week,' he said.

He was not joking, I could see by the very concerned look on his face that he was not happy about it. 'Admittedly, there were no sheep in the field but you never know what some people will get up to these days,' he said.

'You *are* worrying me now,' I said.

'I don't want to do that, but it's there,' he said, and took another swig of his pint.

He worried me more than I cared to let him see, and on my way home from the Black Horse I checked the sheep. They were fine but seemed surprised to see me at that time of night – Jenny 2nd looked at me as if to say, 'What are you doing here?'

The sheep settled into the field well. I was again busy with my school work – mountains of paperwork as usual – as well as looking after all the other farm livestock. We had recently bought four Hereford × Friesian calves, two bulls and two heifers. They were a week old and they were firm favourites with many of the pupils.

Another week passed, and this particular Thursday I had had a hard and tiring day at school. I was going to the Black Horse at about 9 pm for a drink but I looked out of the window to see a very black night indeed. Heavy storm clouds blotted out the moon and stars. The wind howled and the rain lashed down and beat upon the windows.

'Tho' nights be dull and ways be foul

Then nightly sings the staring owl' wrote Shakespeare. Well, the blooming owl could sing to himself. I was not venturing out in that lot. I was afraid the Black Horse would have to do without my patronage that night. At last, I thought, I can get an early night.

True to my word, I lay snuggled under the duvet and listened to the wild antics going on outside. I was grateful to be indoors and I was also pleased we had worked so hard to get the new building erected. If this was October, what did January have in store?

At 1.30 in the morning the telephone rang. I picked up the receiver.

'Hello, is that Mr Terry?' It was a lady's voice.

'It is,' I replied. I was still half-asleep and not quite sure who I was. What could she want at this hour?

'My name is Betty Wilkes, and you teach my daughter Rachel.'

'Yes I do,' I replied, thinking to myself, I hope she isn't ringing to ask for some more homework or something of that nature.

'I'm on my way home from a dinner dance. I'm telephoning you from a callbox on the A5. We have just passed the field with your sheep in it. I know they are yours because Rachel had pointed them out to us.'

'Yes?' I queried, still puzzled by the call.

'Well the bad news is, Mr Terry, that they have got out and at least eight or nine have been killed on the road. Most are lying on the grass verge but one or two are lying in the gutter.'

'Oh no,' I moaned.

'Yes. It's a filthy night and visibility is very bad indeed. The wind is so strong it takes your breath away and it's throwing it down with rain. I should think a large lorry has hit them. I could see a lot of what I think is blood on one sheep's back.'

I was stunned.

'Are you sure?' I asked, almost in a whisper –

hoping she would say that she had had a drop to drink and this was a sick joke.

'Yes, of course I'm sure – we didn't stop. My husband can't stand the sight of blood. We thought it best to telephone you straight away.'

I was wide awake now.

'Thank you for your trouble,' I said.

'That's all right. I just hope you can sort things out,' she said, and put down the receiver.

I started to get dressed but I could not get into my clothes quickly enough. I was terrified. My heart pounded and I felt sick. It sounded as if half the flock had been killed. That was not a road accident, it was a massacre. My old favourites were in that field – Hawthorn Jenny 2nd, Hawthorn Susie and, of course, Randy Dandy. It had taken me since 1979 to build the flock up and now it sounded as if it had been decimated. Mrs Wilkes could be mistaken but I doubted it. They were an intelligent family; he was a chartered accountant and she owned a large shop in town.

I did not bother to do all the buttons up on my shirt – I did not have the time. I put my best trousers on in my haste. Oh well, too bad – if they got dirty they got dirty. I put on an old jumper and a coat.

I was in two minds whether to get someone to help me – but who? I could not telephone my pupils at that hour, their parents would never let them come. Richard Jonas would help and so would Matt Corbutt. I decided to go it alone for the time being, and maybe telephone them later.

I opened the back door and almost got knocked off my feet. It was one of the worst nights I can remember.

The wind was bitterly cold and gale force. The rain was violent and it was very, very dark. I started the engine of the car – the wipers on fast speed were scarcely fast enough. As I drove to the scene I tried to work things out in my mind.

I knew it would be difficult getting the live sheep back into the field, they could have strayed over a mile by now . . . sheep can run fast when they are frightened. The lights and the traffic would surely panic them; some had obviously run into the road, but how long ago? If a large lorry had hit them the driver would probably have stopped and reported it to the police. Surely, if the police had been informed they would have telephoned the owners of the field – the Jonas family – and they would have telephoned me. If a car had been involved, or two or three cars, the first priority would be the safety of the passengers and drivers. Some may even now have been taken to hospital. The last thought on anyone's mind at this stage would be the owner of the sheep.

At every turn in the road I expected to be confronted by blue flashing lights, ambulances, police cars and carnage. We were insured with the National Farmers Union, but that was little comfort at the moment. It would take some sorting out. Probably months or even years. Matt Corbutt's words came back to me: 'I had an electric fencer unit stolen last week'. If someone had stolen ours and death and destruction were the end result, then I hoped whoever had taken it would never sleep easy again. I could be jumping the gun. In these foul conditions perhaps the wind had blown the fence down. . . . If it was my fault the sheep had got out, then it would also be my fault they had caused an accident. . . . If anyone had been badly injured or killed? If . . . if . . . if . . . all the time buzzing in my head like an angry wasp. If . . . if . . . if. . . .

Fallen branches littered the roads and my wind-screen wipers were still doing overtime – so was my imagination. I hoped, but I knew it was not going to be a pretty sight. I kept thinking the worst. Any minute now I would come upon the scene, see the blue flashing lights and a long hard court case would follow.

I had been too independent. Here I was driving along – on my own – to find Heaven knows what awaiting me. I had been a complete fool thinking I could handle this by myself. I should have telephoned someone for help. How would I get the sheep back? I would just have to try and drive them in to the nearest field and hope for the best, and try to get them back next day. But if I did that the field I put them in would probably have gaps in the hedge leading back on to the A5. What a mess I was in!

I was getting nearer and nearer to the field. It was not far now. My heart was thumping quicker and quicker, the adrenalin was flowing and I was shaking, partly with cold and partly with fear. I could not get to the field quick enough, but I dare not drive with any sort of speed because of the terrible road conditions. The vehicles in front were driving slowly and it would be impossible to overtake them – it would be madness to try. It was a good job this traffic was in front of me, otherwise I might have been tempted to put my foot down.

At last I arrived at the corner of the field but I could see nothing yet. Then – I saw it – a sheep

192

lying dead on the grass verge. So it was true, not just a dreadful nightmare. I did not dare to park the car on this road on a night like this. It was bad enough in the daytime in good weather; in these conditions and in total darkness it was asking for trouble. I parked the car on the grass verge, fine for now but whether or not I would be able to move it again later was open to question because I felt the wheels sink a good few inches into the soft soil. I left the headlights on and took my torch. As I got out of the car I spotted another sheep . . . and another . . . and another. . . . They all looked dead. The previous year's show team were in that flock and I felt devastated.

One sheep, I could see, had a lot of blood on its back and it looked as if quite a lot of wool was missing. It was just as Mrs Wilkes had said. But, the sheep looked an unusual shape. It was too flat and, as my eyes focused , it looked as if the sheep had been run over by a steam roller. There was no body shape to it.

I ran to the first one – it was just a sheep skin. I touched it and even picked up the soaking wet pelt. I ran to the second; it too was a sheep skin, the back was bloody – they were untreated skins. I picked one up and moved it out of the gutter. I walked along and picked another out of the gutter; further on there was another one. These last two were very dirty from the traffic. The skins were cold. It did occur to me that perhaps someone had killed our sheep and skinned them, taking just the carcasses. I thought it highly unlikely that they were ours but in that light I could not positively identify them. It was more likely that they had literally fallen off a lorry. Obviously the driver had not missed them because there were no vehicles parked near-by.

The rain was lashing down and I was getting soaked but I was not going home until I had checked my sheep. I would not sleep if I left without looking at them.

I touched the electric fence – and got quite a strong shock off it. I swore to myself, but at least I knew the fence was working. It was too dark for me to see the sheep, and when I called them they could not hear me above the howling wind and rain. Then I saw one of them in the beam of my torch. It was Bella. 'Come on,' I called. 'Come on.' Within seconds I was surrounded. I counted nineteen. True, there should have been twenty-five, including Randy-Dandy. I could see him, but I could not see the others in the dark. The sheep thought they were going to get some supper – but sorry girls, no such luck. I started to walk back to the car and spotted the other six sheep all safe – what a relief! It was obvious the skins really had fallen off the back of a lorry and the driver had not noticed.

I climbed back over the gate and remembered with some alarm that I had left the headlights on. I hoped I had not drained the battery. I was pleased now that I had not telephoned anyone for help – they would have thought me a right idiot.

I counted a total of sixteen sheep skins scattered around. They would have to stop there; I did not want wet, dirty skins in my car. Anyway, if I picked them up I might be accused of stealing them.

I got back in the car, switched off the lights and turned the ignition key. The engine roared into life; all I had to do now was get the car out of the mud. I eased it forward. She moved. Jubilation! We were back on the A5 on my way home.

I went the long way round rather than risk a U-turn with the volume of traffic the A5 carries. The journey back was very different from the outward one. I was very wet, but elated. The sheep were safe.

The whole nightmare had taken approximately twenty minutes from beginning to end – but it is a twenty minutes I never want to go through ever again.

I then stopped and thought for a moment. Life with school children and farm animals was not usually as hair-raising and frightening as this; it was certainly not dull, however. I was enjoying life and I was looking forward to some more enjoyable times. I was sure there would be plenty of them.